Still Standing After All the Tears

STRENGTH · SELF-LOVE · MEANING · FAITH · DECIDE · ATTITUDE · CONTROL · STAND UP · FOCUS ™

Putting Back the Pieces

After All Hell Breaks Loose

Valerie Silveira

STILL STANDING AFTER ALL THE TEARS

Published by: The Rockin' Redhead Group

ISBN 978-0-9861104-0-5

Cover Illustration by: Svetlana Dragicevic

To my son Sean,

You too have suffered pain and heartbreak as a result of your sister's Beast. You *lost* your first friend, your only sibling. I wish I could repay you for the years you stepped aside while my focus was on your sister. Forgive me if you ever felt you were second place in my heart. Thank you for trying to understand how hard it is for a mama bear to let go of her cub, and for letting me know all the time how much I mean to you. I'm proud of you for standing strong in spite of the circumstances, and hope I don't love you *more than you know*. Without you in my world, I'm not sure I would have found the courage to stand up and fight.

I love you,
Mom

Author's Disclaimer

This publication is not intended as a substitute for the advice of a healthcare professional.

My personal story has been told to the best of my recollection. Individual conversations and events were combined or condensed in order to stay on point. The names of most of the individuals have been changed, including my daughter, whom I choose to call "Jordan," out of respect for her story.

Credit has been given to the author of quotes to the best of my ability. Many quotes are attributed to multiple sources, revised, or repeated so many times the original source of the quote may not be known.

I tend to use metaphors in everyday speech and storytelling, and have found that they are incredibly relatable for this subject matter. Therefore, I have chosen to use a few of them in my written works.

I reference my inability to save my daughter from herself and that we cannot save other people. In these instances, I am referring to adults who understand their actions and choices.

I apologize in advance for my lack of perfect grammar, or if my writing style wouldn't earn me an "A" in English class. It's more important to me that I connect with people who need help, than to write perfectly.

Acknowledgements

Over the past thirteen years, the number of people who have made it possible for my heart to heal, and for my message to have meaning, is staggering. Listing each person would take an entire book.

Rich, you're my best friend; the only person this side of heaven with any real understanding of my road to hell and back. You sat *behind* me on the Roller Coaster From Hell, never once wavering in your love. I'm even grateful for the times you were the pin to my balloon; it helped me to grow. There is no earthly way to thank you. I love you.

Svetlana Dragicevic, you're the most amazing artist. You have helped someone who can only draw stick people (bad ones) to bring her artistic side to life.

To my big crazy family; I wouldn't be the woman I am today without each one of you. I don't know if a heart could love a family more than mine does. Had I set out into the world to handpick my family, I would have returned with each one of you.

To the friends (many of whom are family) who have stood by me, I'm grateful to each of you. Thank you for wisdom, encouragement, laughter, and love. Without you in my Circle of Strength, I may have become the old woman in the cave.

For those who have bravely shared their journey with me, I'm honored. Thank you for trusting me with your hearts and allowing me to be part of your story.

Thank you to Sandy Chiupka, Sean Maher, Raphael Eisenberg, and Rod Chiupka for your support far beyond the book.

Thank you to Mishael Patton and Katie Rogers. If not for you, there is no doubt my book would still be rolling around in my head and on reams of disjointed papers. Thank you for your coaching, support, and encouraging me to share my message.

I am grateful to my editors: Rich Silveira, Lynn Chiupka, and Hunter Deiglmeier for reading, and re-reading, editing and correcting. All while I stopped, rearranged, trash canned, and started over. It was not only a creative process, but one that required a few tissues. Thanks for hanging in there with me; it has been a long time since English class. Each of you made this book better.

A Special Note to Women

Women are not traditionally equated with the words "battle," "fight," "Beast," or even "courage." Many of us shy away from violent movies or television shows. Very often, it is women who are the peacemakers in families and other relationships.

One of my personal missions is to live in peace, but I have come to understand that to get there, you often have to go through a Beast. It is time to call this what it is - a battle, a fight.

Women are more than capable of battle. Some of the toughest, most courageous people I know are women. You, my dear sisters are warriors.

What is a Beast?

Beasts come in all shapes and sizes. Some arrive as a result of an alcoholic or addict in the family, abuse, abandonment, an accident or illness, loss, perfectionism, or something else. Many are a combination of two or more. A Beast is a situation, person, attitude, or circumstance that has left you lost, defeated, frustrated, angry, hopeless and helpless, or living in paralyzing fear.

Our Beasts remind us of the past, keep us from living in the present, and fearful of the future.

Introduction

In August 2004, my only daughter suffered a near-fatal gunshot wound, at the hands of her ex-boyfriend, a gang member.

Three years prior to the shooting, Jordan made her way from our safe, comfortable suburban life, into another world. We spent those three years leading up to the shooting, attempting to get her off her collision course. In the hospital after the shooting, I stayed by Jordan's side nearly twenty-four hours a day. Laying in the dark one night in my makeshift bed pressed up against her hospital bed, my eighteen-year-old daughter asked, "Mommy, will you pray with me?"

She had never asked me to pray before, and frankly I'm not very comfortable praying out loud, but that night I held her hand and prayed my heart out. Afterward, it felt as if our nightmare would end, but it was far from over. I would need to put on my seatbelt and strap down my shoulder harness. My ride on the Roller Coaster From Hell was about to get a lot worse.

It would take a few years into the ride to confirm what I had suspected, Jordan was a drug addict. Today she is addicted to heroin.

1

As any parent would, I tried everything I knew in an attempt to save Jordan from her drug addiction Beast. I put on my Supermom Cape and came to her rescue time and time again. My help never moved Jordan closer to battling her Beast, but I couldn't stop trying to save her. The further her life spiraled downward; the further mine spiraled into darkness.

My Beast is a two-headed monster. Not only was I an enabler, but my happiness and sense of purpose had become dependent upon my daughter's willingness to battle her Beast. I was a codependent.

The best way I know how to describe nearly thirteen years of my life is that I was shoved, kicking and screaming onto a roller coaster with my Codependent Enabler Beast by my side. I rode it painfully up one hill and screaming down the next, trapped in a cycle of a mother's hope and suffocating disappointment. With every twist and turn, fear gripped me, and I held on for dear life.

The ride took me through health issues, a web of lies, financial stress, and a broken family. I rode through a world I never wanted to know, the legal system, failed rehabs for Jordan, a serious strain on my marriage, and constant emotional pain.

No matter what the consequences were to my health, finances, or marriage, I continued to strap on the Supermom Cape, choosing to believe the lies and accept the deceit. I covered my ears and eyes and tried to convince myself "this time it was different." At the core of my actions were love and fear. I desperately wanted my baby back, and I was terrified of what might happen if I pulled out the safety net, if I took off the Supermom Cape.

It seemed *everybody else's kids* were doing well while I was living every parent's worst nightmare - losing a child, over and over again. My heart was shattered into a million pieces, standing helplessly as my precious daughter lost herself to drug addiction, despite how much I tried to help her. There was no closure and no way to heal. I was stuck. The world was turning without me, without Jordan, without us. With each failed attempt at saving her, I convinced myself I was a colossal failure as a parent; the part of me I valued most.

One day I asked myself the same question I had asked Jordan many times, "Where is your rock bottom?"

It was then that I realized a simple truth - if I had the ability to save Jordan from herself, from her Beast, I would have done it long ago. I had hit my rock bottom.

The Supermom Cape didn't detach without pain, but I removed it; I stopped enabling Jordan. The codependency part of my Beast didn't go down as easily. My heart ached for my daughter whose twenties were slipping into the past while she was lost in the belly of her Beast. I missed Jordan every second of every day.

Eventually, I began to accept that my best days were behind me. I was a victim who had been unfairly handed a "life sentence." I was at my lowest point, about to give up, when I made a decision that quite possibly saved my life. I decided to Stand Up and Battle My Beast. I share my very painful and personal journey that shattered my heart into a million pieces, and the actions I took to put those pieces back together.

Since I am the mother of a drug addict, some of what you read will be from that perspective. If you are a mother of an addict, this book is for you. If you have a family member or loved one who is an addict, this book is for you. If you are an addict, this book may be for you - it will help you to understand why it seems at times, that your loved one is crazy.

If your Beast has nothing to do with addiction, this book is still for you. No matter what Beast you have been living with, the Nine Actions to Battle Your Beast could mean the difference between living and really **living.**

Part I: When All Hell Broke Loose

"Therefore, rejoice, oh Heavens, and you will live in the Heavens, rejoice.

But terror will come on the earth and the sea

for the devil has come down to you in great anger

knowing that he has little time."

(Revelation 12:12)

Jordan's Been Shot

It was a sunny morning in August of 2004. I got into my car from a breakfast meeting and headed toward home. We lived in Bellevue, Washington, a suburb of Seattle. I retrieved a voice message from my husband Rich and dialed his number.

When he answered the phone, I proceeded to tell him about the meeting, but he cut me off and asked when I would be home. I mentioned that I was going to stop for ingredients for the enchiladas I was making for the cousin party that evening.

Three days prior, our family, and good friends had gathered for a surprise 70th birthday party for my dad. Although Jordan, her brother Sean, and their cousins were teenagers, I was hosting a "cousin party," just as I had many times when they were young. My parents lived in California but were staying an extra day to join the festivities.

I told Rich that although I needed to stop at the store, I was very tired. For some reason, the night before I had tossed and turned, unable to sleep for more than an hour at a time. I was about to learn why.

Rich suggested that I go home and take a nap and go to the store later. I agreed, and a few minutes later, I pulled into the garage.

When the garage door opened, I noticed Rich's car was there. It was a Tuesday, so he should have been at the office. Only minutes before he hadn't let on that he was at home, in fact, he had used the words "go home," rather than "come home." My first thought was that he was going to surprise me and stay home from work that day. I smiled to myself.

As I opened the door and stepped out of my car, Rich emerged from the house. The look on his face told me something was wrong; my heart leaped into my throat. I knew in an instant that I would not be having a nap. There would be no cousin party and no enchiladas.

"Jordan's been shot. He finally shot her Val."

My brain struggled to comprehend what my husband had said. Was it possible that Jordan had been shot? Rich said *he* shot her, and I knew instantly who "he" was. It was her ex-boyfriend, who I refer to as "The Guy."

I shook my head. "No. No. No."

Rich put his arms around me, but I broke free and whimpered, "No. No. No."

He closed the driver side door of my car and gently steered me toward the passenger door of his car.

"Get in. We need to get to the hospital."

"Is she alive?" I cried.

"Yes, but we need to go right now!"

I struggled to free my arm from his grip. I heard his words but didn't want to believe them. I would not get into the car, for fear if I did, this would really be happening.

"Is she alive?" I asked him this question repeatedly.

Each time, he reassured me she was alive, and each time he insisted we needed to get to the hospital.

Eventually, I allowed my husband to pour me into his car, sobbing and gasping for breath.

"Where is she?" I asked, barely able to speak.

"Harborview," Rich replied.

In the Seattle area, Harborview Medical Center was known as the trauma hospital. Nobody ever wanted to hear that someone had been admitted to the emergency room at Harborview.

"Greg called me a couple of hours ago, but you were at the meeting, and I didn't want you to hear about this while you were on the road. He's already there."

"I should've been there." I cried.

Her dad was with her, but I wasn't.

"Where was she shot?" I asked as we raced toward Seattle.

"She was shot in the butt."

The rear end, I thought. How bad can that be? Maybe it was just a flesh wound. I stopped crying and took in deep breaths, trying to steady my breathing. My hands and voice were shaking uncontrollably.

It seemed as if it took forever, but eventually Rich pulled up to the sidewalk of the hospital, where my mom stood waiting. We held one another and sobbed. Jordan and her grandmother had a very close bond, one that had been strained over the prior three years as Jordan's life had taken a very wrong turn. At that moment, all that mattered was getting to Jordan.

Intensive Care Unit

We raced through the hospital and down to the basement to a secondary Intensive Care Unit since the main ICU was full. There was no shortage of trauma patients at Harborview.

I rushed into the ICU and to her bed, stopping for a brief second as I took in the scene. Her dad, her uncle Darryl and her cousin Shawnie were at her bedside. Neither Darryl nor Shawnie worked or lived anywhere close to Seattle, yet they had arrived at the hospital before I had, before her mom.

It flashed through my mind that someone should have gotten me out of the breakfast meeting, but I shook it off and went to Jordan.

Her chest rose and fell, as oxygen pushed into her lungs with the help of a breathing tube. Intravenous lines protruded from her arms and hand. Her face appeared swollen to me, but she looked peaceful, perhaps more so than she had in some time. I kissed my daughter and held her hand, tears dripping from my face.

Shortly after I arrived, the surgeon joined us in the ICU.

"She suffered a GSW to the abdomen."

"She had a GS-what?" I asked.

"A gunshot wound to the abdomen."

"Wait, I thought she was shot in the rear end. What do you mean the abdomen?" I was confused.

"It was an abdominal gunshot wound that entered through her buttock. There's no exit wound."

"You mean the bullet is still inside her?"

"Yes."

"Why didn't you get the bullet out?" I asked.

He looked at me as if I had asked the question in a foreign language.

"You don't understand; gunshot wounds to the abdomen are fatal. We spent hours trying to stop the bleeding, and repairing vessels and veins. We weren't trying to get the bullet out; we were trying to save her life."

The surgeon explained that the bullet had entered from the back at an upward angle next to her tailbone. It traversed her abdomen causing massive internal bleeding. An incision was made from her breastbone all the way down to her pubic bone. My daughter had been filleted open like a fish.

The significant blood loss required transfusions of several units of packed red blood cells. Aside from vascular damage, there was an injury to her internal iliac vein, her left ovary, and the small bowel. I would come to find out later that the bullet barely missed a main artery; an injury that would have caused her to bleed out before she made it to the operating room.

"It's pretty miraculous that the bullet didn't do more damage. She's lucky to be alive," he said.

I thanked the doctor and walked in a semi-trance back to her bedside.

The next several hours were a blur of phone calls, visitors, discussions with the detective and the victim's advocate.

Out of Body Experience

That first day at the hospital, I had one of what would be many "out of body experiences." I don't know how else to explain it other than that. I heard myself tell a friend who had called, "Jordan's been shot." Of course, I had spoken the words, but it didn't seem possible. For an instant, it was as if I was floating above myself. I was a bystander, watching the words flow from my lips.

I have had the same sensation many times in the years since the shooting.

Chaos, Drama, and Terror

We were given a small room just outside the ICU for our family to use. Sometime that morning, Jordan's friend Amanda and her very pregnant sister arrived. They had come from the emergency room where Amanda had been treated for a broken nose and a sprained wrist.

The girls talked breathlessly about the events of the night before. Jordan was at Amanda's apartment in the central district of Seattle, which was a duplex that sat on a hill above the street. Just before 10 PM, they heard very loud music and noticed The Guy's car parked at the end of the road, a place they had never seen him park before. He stood outside of the car with a group of guys.

A couple of days before, The Guy had discovered Jordan and Amanda together and was furious, resulting in The Guy punching Jordan. He was mad that Jordan was hanging out with Amanda, who was also an ex-girlfriend. He was *the man,* and he didn't want his ex-girlfriends talking to each other.

Jordan hid in a bedroom when The Guy walked away from his car and headed toward the apartment. He went in and began ranting about not being invited to the gathering, and wanted to make sure Jordan wasn't there. Satisfied she wasn't, he started to leave when he noticed Jordan peeking out of the bedroom window.

The Guy forced his way back into the apartment and convinced Jordan to open the bedroom door, promising not to hurt her. A verbal argument began, with Amanda jumping into the middle of it. The Guy punched Amanda, knocking her into the bathtub, breaking her nose and spraining her wrist.

Amanda's fifteen-year-old brother brandished a gun, and The Guy left. As he was leaving, The Guy yelled the name of his gang, and they had better remember that the gang "did it." Those words did not mean as much at the time as they would down the road.

A few minutes later, gunfire erupted. Everyone hit the ground, except for Jordan.

For some reason, Jordan was alone in the apartment next door when the shots were fired. Unlike the others, she didn't immediately comprehend what was happening; she wasn't accustomed to hearing gunfire. One of the dozens of bullets fired smashed through the front window and hit Jordan.

Tears streamed down my cheeks as I envisioned Jordan lying in a pool of her own blood.

The chaos and violence the girls re-lived made my head spin. It was no television drama; it was real, and it was happening to my family.

The events of the night before were far from the world that I lived in, or the one in which Jordan was raised. I wanted to cover my ears and run from the room, but at the same time, I was desperate to know anything about the past three years; the life Jordan worked to keep from me.

How Low a Person Can Go

In the afternoon, a boy arrived at the ICU. He wore saggy jeans and an oversized coat. It was a warm summer day, but I was far too preoccupied to question why he was wearing a winter coat. Amanda introduced him as her brother, the boy who had defended Jordan and Amanda the night before.

The trio talked non-stop for hours. I had a splitting headache, so I said goodbye, and we all left the ICU waiting room. I felt a moment of peace, but it was to be short-lived.

Mom and I met up in the cafeteria across the hall from the ICU. We chatted for a moment when Mom realized she left her purse in the ICU waiting room. When she arrived, she discovered that her purse was missing. Gone were her wallet, glasses, sunglasses, credit cards, checkbook, driver's license, insurance cards and more. She was certain the boy with the big coat had stolen it.

It was unfathomable to me that anybody would stoop so low as to steal a purse out of the ICU waiting room, let alone a visitor who had attempted to protect Jordan only hours before. I wanted to believe that a stranger or hospital worker was responsible.

Mom spent the next couple of hours canceling credit cards, alerting banks and making a police report while her granddaughter laid in the ICU with a breathing tube in her mouth and a bullet in her belly.

We would learn a few days later that mom was right. The boy wearing the big coat was caught using her credit card at a gas station.

Stuff You Don't Really Want to Know

9-1-1, What Is Your Emergency?

When the bullet hit Jordan, she felt a burning sensation in her lower buttock, but she didn't feel any pain.

There was a lot of commotion in the apartment next door and outside the duplex. At first, nobody was aware of Jordan's injury, or too preoccupied to care where she was.

Jordan didn't realize that someone next door had already reported the incident, so she pulled her phone from her pocket and dialed 9-1-1.

Somewhere in the emergency response archives is a call that went something like this:

"911, what is your emergency?"

"I've been shot. Please hurry."

"What is the address?"

Jordan knew the street, but not the house number. She got up, walked outside onto the porch, and read the numbers off to the emergency operator.

She went back into the house, laid down on the floor and waited for help.

The last thing she remembers about that night was asking the EMT if she was going to die.

He replied, "Not in my truck."

The last thing the EMT reported was that she had lost a lot of blood, was vomiting, and going into shock.

It Doesn't Work Like a Crime Drama

A lone detective was assigned to the case. The first day after the shooting, the detective was already frustrated. Although there were two shooters, he was convinced he knew who had shot Jordan and wanted him arrested ASAP. He wasn't sure where The Guy was, or how many search warrants they would need in order to find him or the gun.

We both understood that unless The Guy were arrested immediately, the gun would likely be at the bottom of Lake Washington.

Search warrants and arrest warrants don't magically appear as they do on television. They take time. Due to his gang affiliation and the nature of the crime, the arrest would be handled carefully.

As the day wore on, the detective was becoming more and more frustrated as evidenced by his comment,

"It's called the criminal justice system because the justice is for the criminals!"

He explained that two types of bullet casings were found outside the house where the shooting occurred. They were 9-mm and 40 calibers. I had heard those terms before, but only in books and movies. He said that there were an "unbelievable number of bullet casings" on the street below the duplex. It appeared The Guy and his friend didn't just shoot a few rounds at the house; they had re-loaded. Eyewitnesses placed The Guy at the spot on the street next to the pile of 9-mm bullet casings.

The Guy, who would claim his innocence up to the bitter end of the legal process, hid out in his mother's house and refused to cooperate with the police. Eventually, a police negotiator was called in to secure The Guy's surrender. He was arrested and eventually charged with nine felony counts, including Attempted Murder in the First Degree.

Just as we had suspected, too much time had passed between the shooting and his arrest. The police never found the gun. There has never been a doubt in my mind that if the gun has not been destroyed, it has been used again.

The second shooter was never identified.

9-mm Bullets

Once Jordan was awake, and the breathing tube removed, she was taken to x-ray in order to locate the bullet.

Rich went to retrieve a few toiletries and a change of clothes for me. Everyone else had gone home for the night. I would be sleeping on the sofa in the now familiar room outside of ICU until Jordan was released to trauma recovery. I had spent less than 12 hours there, yet it seemed as if I had been imprisoned in the tiny windowless room for weeks.

It was the first time I had been alone all day. I sat in silence wondering where it had all gone wrong. The past three years seemed unbelievable. Jordan went from a good student and athlete to a girl heading down a very dangerous path. I wondered how it was that my daughter, who had grown up in a safe and loving home had ended up in a hospital with a bullet stuck in her body. Reality was beginning to set in - my daughter really had been shot.

Her nurse wheeled Jordan back into the ICU.

As he brought her into the room, he declared, "Man, that's a big bullet. Looks like a 9-mm to me."

His comment seemed nonchalant, but I assumed that since he worked in ICU at Harborview, it was not his first gunshot patient. My daughter is the only gunshot patient I have ever known.

Since witnesses placed The Guy where the 9-mm bullet casings were found, it appeared it was The Guy's gun that had fired the bullet now lodged in Jordan's abdomen, near her belly button.

Not the "Type"

A victim's advocate was assigned to Jordan. Misty served as Jordan's voice during the legal process. She attended hearings and kept us updated on legal proceedings. Misty and I were discussing what we both recently learned; Jordan was a victim of domestic violence before the shooting.

Several months prior, Jordan showed up at home with bruises on her upper arms that looked to be fingerprints. When I questioned her about them, she dismissed me quickly, giving a ridiculous explanation about messing around with a friend.

"It doesn't make sense," I told Misty. "Jordan is very strong-willed and confident. She's not the type of person who would let anyone abuse her."

"There is no *type*," Misty replied.

"It's not just the shy, quiet women who find themselves in a cycle of domestic violence. In fact, many times it's the women who do put up a fight. You would be shocked if I told you the number of professionals, doctors and lawyers in this city alone, who abuse their wives," she continued.

"But, I know Jordan," I protested.

At least I thought I knew her. She had never witnessed domestic violence in my home or her dad's home. Jordan grew up knowing it was never acceptable for a guy to lay hands on her. I recall telling Jordan that if a guy ever hit me, he had better make it a good one because he wouldn't get a second chance. I assumed Jordan was like me. It was looking more and more as if Jordan was nothing like me.

After Misty had left, I wondered how much more I would learn about Jordan's life; how many times my heart would break before the end, whatever that would be.

People Are Not As Honest as You Think

I could not seem to get my head wrapped around the fact that somebody could stoop so low as to steal the purse of a grieving grandmother.

When it was confirmed that the boy with the baggy coat stole the purse, I was reminded of an encounter two decades prior. I worked for a startup company, and as we began to expand the executive and management staff, we implemented a psychological testing policy. I was already on board, so I wasn't scheduled for testing. However, the psychologist agreed to administer the test for me and to go over it in detail.

I was impressed; the test nailed even the most complex parts of my personality. As he explained certain results, I would recall particular questions from the test that would have led to those conclusions.

When the psychologist came to one area on the graph, he made a statement I will never forget.

"You think people are a lot more honest than they are."

My mind was racing; going back over the questions that may have led to that statement. One particular question came to mind - a scenario was presented in which a person could gain access to a large sum of money with a guarantee that nobody would ever find out. The question was worded something like this, "would *most* people do it?" To my logical brain, *most people* translated to 51%. I was certain most people would not take the money. I explained my conclusion to him and said,

"It can't be true."

"It's true," he said. "Most people would take the money."

When I was eight years old, I learned from a friend that there was no Santa Claus. In an instant, I realized that not only was Santa a lie, but so were the Easter Bunny and the Tooth Fairy. I was crushed.

I don't know if the psychologist's statement is true, or if there is any way to know for sure. What I did know is that I didn't want to accept that I was living in a world where most people are dishonest.

It was sad when I learned about Santa. The day the psychologist told me that people are not as honest as I thought they were my world was rocked a little bit.

When the boy stole my mother's purse from the ICU waiting room, my faith in humanity took a serious blow.

Mommy, Will You Pray With Me?

As soon as her condition stabilized, Jordan was moved to a section of the hospital for trauma recovery. Since she was a victim of a violent crime, thanks to an advocate at the hospital, she was given a private room so I could stay with her. A hard, worn out recliner chair would be my bed for more than a week.

During the hospital stay, for the most part, Jordan was distant and demanding. I chalked it up to pain and fear. After all, she had been shot, and there were nearly 50 staples holding her gut together.

Although she wanted me in the room every second and insisted my chair be pressed up against her hospital bed, she wouldn't share with me her thoughts or feelings. I was desperate to re-bond with the daughter that I was losing.

One night as we lay side by side in the dark, Jordan told me what happened the night of the shooting. It aligned with what Amanda and her sister told me. It was the story the detective had pieced together. Moreover, it was the story she would tell the prosecutor's office when they visited the hospital to take her statement. When she finished, she quietly asked,

"Mommy, will you pray with me?"

Jordan had never asked me to pray before, nor has she since. I'm not very comfortable praying out loud, but that night I held her hand and prayed my heart out. I cried silent tears of joy and thanked God for bringing Jordan back to me.

Afterward, it felt as if our nightmare would end, but it was far from over. I would need to put on my seatbelt and strap down my shoulder harness. My ride on the Roller Coaster From Hell was about to get a lot worse.

The Roller Coaster From Hell

Motion sickness has plagued me my entire life and prevented me from enjoying most amusement park rides, except for roller coasters. That was the one ride that didn't make me sick. However, several years ago, they too, began to make me nauseous. My amusement park days were over. I stopped riding roller coasters altogether – or so I thought.

One might assume that my ride on the Roller Coaster From Hell started the day Jordan was shot, but the reality is that I had been shoved onto the roller coaster three years prior. It seemed that one day she was a thriving, happy girl, getting good grades, and playing select sports, and the next day, a fifteen-year-old teenager hell-bent on self-destruction.

Losing Jordan

Jordan met some girls through a golf professional we knew, and although she belonged to a church youth group, she wanted to participate with them in their youth outreach program in nearby Tacoma. The group operated an underage hip-hop club as a way to reach out to at-risk youth. Those attending the club were patted down at the doors, and they were not allowed to wear gang colors or clothing. The idea was to provide a safe place for them to go, where they would receive a positive message.

I reluctantly allowed her to participate. One day Jordan told me about a boy she had met there. I questioned her and eventually figured out he was not part of the youth outreach group, but one of the kids in attendance! Of course, we no longer allowed her to participate with that particular youth group.

Around that same time, Jordan attended a basketball game at a high school in Seattle. It would turn out to be the basketball game that changed our lives forever.

At first, I didn't know she had met The Guy at the game that night. I just knew her behavior began to change drastically. The once responsible girl became lazy, unmotivated, and deceitful. She took our car before she had a license and drove it at night, in the snow. She ran away from home and got into trouble with the law.

Jordan had always been popular and a good student, but suddenly she didn't like her school. We registered her in a new school, but after a few months, she was unhappy there. At the age of sixteen, she quit high school, and I became certified as a home schoolteacher.

Jordan is a natural athlete. From a very young age, she played softball, soccer, and basketball. She played on a select softball team and the high school team. Then, she stopped playing sports altogether.

When we found out about The Guy, we forbid her to have contact with him. I had figured out pretty quickly that The Guy was bad news. I voiced my concern to Jordan that he probably carried a gun and was in a gang. She reacted as if I were crazy. A call from him, while he was in juvenile hall increased my concern. I found some letters from him, instructing her as to whom she could and could not speak to and telling her to send him money.

We couldn't seem to keep her from The Guy, or his world. I took her to see a counselor in town, but she ended up manipulating the counselor.

I took her to speak with the youth pastor and another pastor at our church who were well acquainted with the area of Seattle where The Guy lived and very familiar with that world.

"You don't know this world," one of them told her.

"He's different," Jordan insisted.

He told her, "I could line up 20 girls right now from that world, all with babies, and all with the baby daddy in prison. And each one of them said he was *different*."

"You don't know him," she said in defiance.

He told her, "You think because you listen to a little hip-hop music that you know this world? You have no idea what you are getting yourself into; trust me. I know this world; you don't."

She wouldn't listen and ended up quitting youth group.

Jordan was unwilling to live by our house rules and went to live with her dad. It broke my heart that our relationship had come to that point, but was hopeful that time and distance would repair the relationship that was unraveling at an alarming rate.

No matter how suspicious I was, I couldn't get Jordan to tell me what was going on with her. Until she was ready to come clean, I was left to wonder if my suspicions of alcohol or drug use were true. Or, if what she accused me of was the truth, that she wasn't doing anything wrong. The problem was that I "just think too much."

One thing was for certain; there had to be a reason the smartest person I knew was now a girl I barely knew anymore.

I Choose Him

We stood in our kitchen one afternoon in a heated conversation. It was one of many that started with me trying to convince Jordan that her relationship with The Guy was bad for her in every way.

"Are you asking me to choose between the family and him?" Jordan screamed.

"I guess that is exactly what I'm saying, Jordan. We don't want him in our world."

The look on Jordan's face is forever imprinted in my memory. I thought at any moment, little horns might pop through her hair and fire spew from her mouth. Her eyes were dark and cold.

"Then I choose him!" she yelled.

It was at that moment I recognized something different about Jordan. As she stared me down, I had the eerie feeling that someone or something else was looking back at me.

I Don't Like the Way They Make Me Feel

When Jordan was released from the hospital, she came to stay in her old room. The walls were still a shade of orange she had picked out when she was twelve. For over a month, I slept with her. I wanted to be there as she recovered from major surgery, and she wanted me there because she had become terrified of the dark. We slept with a light on every night.

One morning, I awoke to hear Jordan in the bathroom. I found her standing over the toilet with the bottle of pain medication she had been prescribed, ready to dump them down the toilet.

"I don't like the way they make me feel," she said.

Before I could stop her, she dumped them into the toilet and flushed them away. Jordan never took another pain pill during her recovery from the shooting.

The irony wasn't lost on me when years later, I would learn Jordan's addiction began with the same opiate.

As If It Never Happened

Approximately six weeks after the shooting, I was in the kitchen getting dinner ready when Jordan came through, headed for the garage. She had her purse over one shoulder and a tote bag over the other.

"I'm going back to my dad's now."

I was speechless for a few moments, before rattling off a series of questions and statements, such as:

"Why are you leaving?"

"What about your health?"

"You're not completely healed yet."

"We need to get you some counseling."

She waved off everything I said, and continued toward the door.

"I'm fine, mom. See you later. Love you."

The girl who slept with her mom in a lighted room for nearly six weeks walked out the door as if nothing had happened.

An Unlikely Witness

The prosecutor called and asked, "Would you be willing to come to court and tell the truth?"

I said, "Of course I will tell the truth, but what about?"

He told me that upon leaving home, Jordan had gone straight to his office and recanted the statement she had given in the hospital.

He relayed that The Guy had made threatening phone calls to all of the witnesses, including Jordan. The Guy was allowed phone privileges but was not to contact witnesses. The three-way-calls were facilitated by his mother.

Although Jordan denied it, the prosecuting attorney was convinced she recanted because she too had been threatened.

I asked him, "What is it you want me to tell the court? Obviously I wasn't there."

He said, "I need you to tell the jury what Jordan told you in the hospital about the night of the shooting."

"So, basically you are asking me to go to court and testify that Jordan is now lying."

"Yes," he answered, "will you do it?"

I questioned Jordan about the phone calls, and she laughed it off. She insisted that not only had The Guy not threatened her, but that she couldn't even remember what had happened the night of the shooting. She was no longer sure it was The Guy who had fired the bullets. He wouldn't hurt her, not on purpose.

I was furious at her for defending The Guy, and I agreed to testify.

For making the threatening phone calls, The Guy was placed in solitary confinement for the remainder of his stay in the county jail.

Losing Faith in the Justice System

Several months after the shooting, jury selection was complete. The prosecutor felt the selection process had gone well. I had seen many jury selections on television and in movies, but had never sat on a jury. Jury selection, I learned, was one of the most critical factors in a trial.

In this case, certain facts related to The Guy would not be allowed at the trial, so as not to prejudice the jury against him. For one, the judge denied the prosecutor's request to make the jury aware of The Guy's gang affiliation. Recall, The Guy proudly announced right before the shooting that it was his gang that "did it." He made sure to connect what was about to happen, directly to his gang. Now he and his attorney were working hard to keep that fact from the jury.

Further, the jury would be precluded from learning of his nine felonies as a juvenile.

I was beyond disappointed that the jury was not able to see the pattern of behavior of The Guy. Nor would they fully understand the character of a person who had assaulted two young women, opened fire on a house full of people with no regard for human life, and had nearly taken Jordan's life.

They would be prevented from knowing The Guy was unable to make the very high bail that had been set, and therefore was in custody. The jury was not to see him in a county jail-issued jumpsuit. Bailiffs were instructed to bring The Guy into the courtroom well in advance of the jury and to make sure the jury had left the courtroom well in advance of handcuffing The Guy.

During pre-trial proceedings, the judge introduced The Guy to the jury as the gentleman wearing a certain color shirt. The Guy shot back at the judge, correcting her on the color of the shirt, which was his gang color. The same judge who had disallowed the gang affiliation changed her mind. They would now be made aware of The Guy's gang membership.

Apparently, whether or not a jury is privy to certain information regarding a defendant is predicated on how the judge is feeling at any given moment.

In any case, the prosecuting attorney was relieved that the gang affiliation had been allowed and felt the trial was off to a promising start. However, the process went sideways when news reached the judge that some members of the jury may have seen The Guy being led from the courtroom in handcuffs. The jury was dismissed, and the selection process would start over.

It had been nearly nine surreal months since the shooting, and now it would drag out further. I was eager to close this chapter of our nightmare.

Since the shooting, I had lived in fear and apprehension in the home where I once felt safe. We didn't know whether we were in danger. Regardless, the day before Jordan was shot was the last day I ever felt safe and secure in that home.

Since I was considered a witness, a security plan was put into place for my safety during the trial. I would be picked up for court and delivered to a private entrance, and then led to and from the private entrance by armed officers.

I never had to testify. Just before the trial was to begin, The Guy accepted a plea bargain. He would take the Alford Plea - not admitting guilt, but stating a jury of his peers would likely find him guilty. He pled to just one of the nine charges, Assault in the First Degree - Domestic Violence.

The prosecutor called me with what he considered *good news*. For the prosecution, the county, the state, the community, this was considered a victory. It was a conviction; it was a win.

The Guy's sentence would be 10 to 14 years.

"If they're taking votes, I vote for 14 years," I told the prosecuting attorney.

He chuckled and went on to explain that I could have an influence on sentencing. If I appeared and explained what The Guy's actions had done to my daughter's life, how it had devastated our family, he would likely get the full 14-year sentence. I told him I would be there.

"Not so fast," he told me.

He went on to explain that the hearing would be open to the public, and it was likely some of his gang friends would be at the back of the courtroom. He expressed concern that I might not make it home that day.

I was stunned. Jordan came close to being murdered by The Guy. My family was devastated as a result of The Guy's actions. I was yanked into a world I never chose to be a part of, yet I did not have the right to safety while explaining that in court. It will never make sense to me that victims aren't allowed the respect of privacy and the guarantee of safety while moving painfully through the legal process.

I lost a tremendous amount of faith in what I once considered the best justice system in the world. I couldn't help but recall what the detective had said in frustration the day after the shooting:

"It's called the criminal justice system because the justice is for the criminals!"

We couldn't turn back the clock and undo what had been done. Each of us would have to find a way to process an ordeal that only months before, was something we could not have imagined.

I never appeared at sentencing, and as expected, The Guy was sentenced to 10 years. Specifically, 129 nine months, less time served. With a sentence reduction for good behavior, he would probably serve nine years in prison. I served more time than that in my own prison.

Supermom to the Rescue

I am convinced that mothers are given an invisible cape to take home with their newborn babies. We use it every time our child needs rescuing, sometimes long after they reach adulthood.

You expect to use the Supermom Cape when your son falls and skins his knee, or when a boy breaks your daughter's heart. It seems perfectly acceptable to use the Cape when your child pulls a high school prank. Never could you imagine your Cape will be used in an attempt to save your children from themselves.

In the years after the shooting, Jordan continued all of the same behavior she had prior to the shooting, and worse. She spent her twenties going from job to job or no job at all. I spent most of her twenties with my Cape on, coming to her rescue. I paid security deposits, rents, car loans, insurance payments, traffic tickets, fines, and medical bills. I bought groceries, clothing, supplements, household items, toiletries, and even perfume! Each time she abandoned her belongings, I bought her more.

I took her to have her ankle bracelet put on and stayed close to her while she wore it for 30 days. I paid for bail bonds and sent money to jails for incidentals and telephone calls. I hired an attorney, paid for drug treatments and drove thousands of miles to retrieve her when she was extradited to another state. And the list goes on.

The point is that I spent tens of thousands of dollars, cried gazillions of tears, and allowed my heart to be shattered into a million pieces, but none of that helped. Jordan and her Beast lied to me and deceived me so many times that I wasn't sure which end was up. Jordan is my daughter, and I didn't know how to stop, so I kept going back for more.

I cried, begged, pleaded, yelled and screamed, threatened to cut her off, and changed my phone number. I swore I would not spend another dime, and then found myself opening up my wallet, one more time.

I had a Supermom Cape, and I wasn't afraid to use it. My husband wanted to rip the Cape off me a hundred times, so I did my best to hide it from him. The woman who stood for integrity was betraying her husband's trust by helping Jordan behind his back. I hated myself for doing it, but convinced myself that I was only protecting him.

Years later, I was heartbroken and worn out, Jordan had not been saved, and I was standing before my husband asking for forgiveness.

In the Belly of Her Beast

One time Jordan contacted me and said she had no food and had not eaten since the day before.

She stood outside of a little house with a short white fence, surrounding an overgrown yard. She had attempted to make herself up, but the smeared black eyeliner and bright lipstick didn't hide her declining physical and emotional health. The white top she wore was wrinkled and should have been in the laundry long ago. Her face was broken out, and she had dirt under her fingernails.

Jordan acted like a kid on Christmas when she saw what was in the big tote bags full of food. A teenage boy walked through the little fence and stood playing with an electronic device. They didn't acknowledge one another. I didn't ask who lived in the house, and she didn't offer.

We said we loved each other, and I drove away as she struggled with the bags. I wanted to slam on my brakes, jump out of the car, and take her with me, far away from that life. I was finally learning to let go, so instead, I drove away blinking back the tears.

Several of my Supermom rescue attempts included Jordan begging me to allow her to stay in our guest suite, promising she was clean and that this time would be different.

Within a day or two she would either disappear or be detoxing. If a detox began, she was unwilling for it to continue. The only option she or her drug Beast would consider was more drugs. I have heard detoxing from heroin can be likened to having the flu, multiplied by 100. Once a detox begins, an addict knows that all it takes is one hit to stop the pain of withdrawal. No wonder the odds of beating a drug Beast are so low.

I want Jordan to beat the odds; I still believe she can. She is one of the strongest willed people I have ever known. Apparently the drug addiction Beast is even stronger willed.

With no choice but to return my adult daughter to her drug world, I would drive at first in silence, glancing over at her while she was sweating and beginning to tremble.

As we turned each corner and crossed through intersections, moving closer to our destination, I would try reasoning with her. No amount of pleading would change her mind. Rehab was not an option. There was, but one option she would consider; with which her Beast would agree.

Each time I dropped her off, she turned to me and told me she loved me, and then got out of the car without much more than the clothes on her back. Through tears, I watched in the rearview mirror, as my beloved Jordan made her way across the street and disappeared into the belly of her Beast.

My Beast

My Codependent Enabler Beast

My Beast is a two-headed monster. Not only was I an enabler, but my happiness and sense of purpose had become dependent upon my daughter's willingness to battle her Beast. I was a codependent. **This is my Beast.**

One definition of codependency is: *"A codependent person is one who has let another person's behavior affect him or her, and who is obsessed with controlling that person's behavior."*[i]

An enabler is defined as *"One who enables another to achieve an end; especially: one who enables another to persist in self-destructive behavior (a substance abuse) by providing excuses or making it possible to avoid the consequences of such behavior."*[ii]

Around and around I went, tortured by what was happening to my daughter, powerless to stop it, and unwilling to move on with my life until it did stop. Clearly, I was living with a Beast.

Shame, Guilt, and Stigma

In anticipation of Jordan choosing rehab, I made some phone calls. One was to a local well-known facility. Most rehabs have sliding scales, so I inquired as to a rate for their program for someone without financial means, and was told it was $10,000. Unfortunately, Jordan didn't have $10. She explained that an option would be another recovery center in a nearby town. Their financial assistance program would be $5,000. She was very complimentary toward the other treatment center and stated that many of their counselors had gone through that very treatment program.

I knew the area where the center was, right smack in the middle of the drug area of that town. I voiced my concern, letting her know I didn't want Jordan around "those kind of people."

She replied, "Your daughter is taking street drugs. She *is one of those people.*"

I nearly fell off my chair. She was right, but it was painful to hear. It wasn't easy to connect the dots between the incredibly gifted Jordan, and the Jordan who was now being described as "one of those people." Not only would I need to accept the fact that my daughter was a heroin addict, but to face the reality that I

48

was the mother of a heroin addict. The shame that I already felt multiplied.

To say I had high hopes for Jordan's life from the time she was a toddler is putting it mildly. Jordan is very intelligent, athletic, artistic, and witty. We measure our parenting success or failure, to a certain degree, based on where our children are in their lives. Our self-worth is tied to our children, and when they make wrong choices, our egos become bruised.

If Jordan was indeed "one of those people," then what kind of a person did that make me? How had I failed so miserably as a parent? I was somehow guilty of something.

More than once, I had been on my soapbox proclaiming that if a child went astray, it was the parents' fault. Maybe this was the source of my guilt. I had judged and condemned parents of criminals and addicts, and those who had simply made some bad choices. I had assumed it was bad parenting. I had summarily discounted both free will, and addiction.

I stood sanctimoniously in judgment of grieving parents, who had lost their children over and over. Then it happened to Jordan, and I fell off my soapbox. I fell hard.

Society makes certain we have a steady stream of shame and guilt, adding stigma, like a cherry on top of our shame and guilt

49

pie. We pile enough shame and guilt on ourselves as parents without anyone adding to it.

We did not choose to have our children become addicts, just as they did not start out in life planning to become addicts. Society will tell parents of addicts that they feel sorry for you, but in another breath they will wonder, "How did you let your kid end up this way?" The stigma that surrounds parents of addicts or those struggling with other issues is suffocating. It is what keeps us in the shadows, rarely reaching out unless it is anonymous.

Several people, upon meeting me or hearing my story have reacted with comments meant to be complimentary toward me. They have said things such as, "I would never have guessed *you* would have an addict for a child."

Their comments were no doubt meant to express their surprise at how well I appear to be doing in spite of the tragic circumstances. No matter, I can't help but wonder if they half-expect me to have a needle sticking out of my arm.

What do the parents of addicts look like? We look like doctors, lawyers, factory workers, accountants, actors, and receptionists. We look like single moms and dads, Boy Scout leaders, loving parents, struggling parents, softball coaches, and Sunday school teachers. We are blondes, brunettes, and redheads. We have black hair or no hair. Most of us have some gray hair.

We come from all socio-economic groups, ethnic backgrounds, and all cultures. What do parents of addicts look like? We look like you.

There is likely some stigma attached to your Beast, whatever that Beast may be. It is easy for others to judge you or to analyze your actions. People may be quick to offer their critique or to disregard the severity of your pain. It is easy to make a critical judgment about another person's Beast without ever having lived with that Beast.

We all need to work together to shed the shame, guilt and stigma attached to our Beasts.

Nobody's Bringing a Casserole

When somebody passes away, it's common for friends and relatives to bring food to the family and loved ones of the person who passed. Not only does it ensure that people eat during their grief, but it is a gesture of compassion and love. When Jordan was released from the hospital after the shooting, my friends Joyce and Sonja each brought us food; they literally brought casseroles.

The casserole I'm referring to in this section is metaphorical for the support people receive after a loss and during the first stages of the grieving process.

Sadly, when your child or loved one is on a path of destruction, you live in a constant state of grief. Each time there is hope, it's followed by a plunge from hope into a devastating state of disappointment, despair, hopelessness, and loss. You live in near-constant grief. In situations of continued loss and grief, nobody is bringing a casserole.

People are unsure what to say or do, or how to act in a situation such as this. Do they bring a casserole every single time your heart breaks?

I could have used a few more *casseroles*, but I failed to tell people I was hungry.

Losing Me

I am a fairly self-confident person by nature, but after so many failed attempts at saving Jordan from herself, my confidence was all but gone. I became solely focused on Jordan. I went through the motions of life, most of it with a smile on my face that only masked my despair.

For years, I awoke each morning and momentarily looked forward to the day. I no sooner wiped the sleep from my eyes, when the realization hit me - this *is* my life. I drug myself out of bed and went through the motions of living.

On some days, I was determined to get better, but any hope I found during the day went down with the sun. Days, weeks, months, and years sped by; faster and faster time seemed to move. Rather than becoming stronger, I was losing ground each day.

Even the people closest to me didn't comprehend the magnitude of my pain; it was a 15 on the Richter scale. Family and friends knew Jordan was shot, and certainly, they understood that Jordan's life was spinning out of control. They heard some of the stories and were eventually made aware that she was addicted to drugs. No doubt, they all felt a certain amount of empathy and sympathy, and those who are parents could only *imagine* the pain of walking the road of addiction with a child.

Even Rich didn't understand the extent of my sadness. I would cry in my walk-in closet, so as not to upset him. He found me in there on a few occasions. Rich witnessed the black cloud descend upon me out of nowhere and watched me fight to stop it.

Most of what I felt 24 hours a day, I kept to myself. First, I didn't know how to describe the overwhelming ache in my heart.

Next, I didn't want to be a burden; for people to feel sorry for me. I was very good at hiding my pain from the world, but I was barely holding it together.

With each milestone that my nieces and nephews reached; graduations, new jobs, college, marriage, children; I was reminded of my loss. Life had become very unfair, and I was fast becoming trapped in victim mode. It may not have shown on the outside, but I was devastated on the inside.

Jordan and one of her cousins had been the best of friends before all hell broke loose. When that cousin was married, it broke my heart that Jordan wasn't in the wedding; she wasn't even at the wedding.

The birth of my grandniece was bittersweet. I was happy for her parents, and for my sister who would have her first grandchild. I was thankful for my family's little miracle. At the same time, I was overcome with sadness. It was on the otherwise joyous day of my grandnieces birth that I presented Jordan with two options: 1) rehab; 2) leaving her grandparents' house and going her own way. She left telling me she would call in three hours; I didn't hear from her for three weeks, and then for months.

It was very difficult to be happy for others when it felt so unfair that I lived on the Roller Coaster From Hell. I tried to focus on the positive and to be happy for others, but the waves of sadness wouldn't stop. As bad as those waves were, the shame and guilt that came crashing in afterward, nearly drowned me.

Life goes on. Life was going on without me. I felt like a stranger in the company of others, even when I was the life of the party. I was putting on a show; that was about to have its last curtain call. I was losing *me*.

People have confided in me over the years that they have considered suicide. It has never even crossed my mind, yet one day I found myself telling Rich,

"I don't want to be here anymore; it's just too hard."

For most of my life, I didn't understand depression. I had never been depressed for more than an hour. That was before I met my Beast. I'm not certain why I didn't recognize the dark cloud for what it was - depression.

Perhaps my ego didn't want to believe I could be a depressed person. After all, I'm strong and happy by nature. It turns out some of the strongest and naturally happy people I know have been through periods of depression.

I tried to explain to my husband a couple of times how alone I felt, but I didn't even understand it myself. He must have been incredibly sad, and confused, not knowing how to help me not to feel alone, when he was standing right there.

Down on the Mat

I was at the point of giving up. Jordan had been shot, in legal trouble, homeless and continuing to poison her body. She was on a collision course towards death. She had not hit rock bottom, and I was terrified of what her rock bottom might be. My life was so intertwined with my daughter's that it felt as if we were drowning together, yet separately. I didn't know what to do anymore. I was exhausted, broken-hearted, and numb. The Beast had all but beaten me. I was beginning not to care one way or the other what happened to me.

This story depicts just how I felt before I decided to stand up and fight.

I was in the ring, lying on my back on the proverbial mat, with my Beast on top of me. I wanted to get up, but I was tired. The referee began the count.

*"**One**," he yelled.*

I reminded myself that regardless of losing Jordan repeatedly, as long as she was alive, there was hope. I lifted my head, determined to free myself from the Beast.

He leaned over me and whispered in my ear, "Jordan doesn't even want to fight, so your life is pretty much over."

I dropped my head back onto the mat and closed my eyes.

*"**Two**," The referee counted.*

I thought about all of the hardship I had endured, even before Jordan's addiction, and yet I had been a survivor. I could do this. I pushed the Beast, but he grabbed my arms and put his face close to mine and said ever so lovingly,

"Some people get to be happy in this life. Sorry sweetheart, but you aren't one of them."

The Beast's claws pinned my arms to the mat. I turned my head away.

*"**Three**," I heard the referee bellow.*

Sean's image came to my mind; he still needed me. I struggled to free my arms from the Beast's grip.

He spoke sharply, "You have failed as a parent; you couldn't save your own daughter."

I stopped clawing at the Beast and flopped back down to the mat. I was becoming exhausted. Maybe the Beast was right, and I had failed my daughter.

*"**Four**," Said the referee as he pounded the mat.*

What had happened to my hopes and dreams, I asked myself. Wasn't there still time for me to make some meaning out of all of this? I pushed the Beast and tried to sit up. He slammed me to the mat, threw his head back and a blood-curdling laugh escaped his mouth.

"What kind of meaning could you possibly make from this? Your daughter is a heroin addict, and you are the mother of a heroin addict, nothing more."

I didn't even attempt to get free.

*"**Five**." The referee counted out loudly.*

I heard Rich encouraging me to get up. I shoved as hard as I could and surprisingly, the Beast fell off me. I sat up, determined to stand.

"Seriously, you think it is right for you to move on without Jordan? What kind of a mother would do that?"

He licked his red lips with his long black tongue and stood staring down at me with piercing yellow eyes. I glared back at him, unable to move.

*"**Six**." The referee slapped the mat.*

I saw my nieces and nephews, my goddaughter and godson, and my sponsor children. Didn't I still matter to them? I got to my knees. My Beast moved in closer.

"You mean nothing to them!"

Tears began to spill from my eyes, as I let out my breath and sat silently on my knees. I wanted to get up more than anything, but I felt defeated in every way.

"**Seven**." The count continued.

My mind was flooded with the lies and deceit of addiction; of Jordan's Beast, and mine. It was time to start taking care of myself. I could find the strength to stand up. I shoved him, and he fell off balance, allowing me to get one foot on the ground before he steadied himself.

"**Eight**," The referee declared excitedly.

Enough was enough. If it were possible to save her from herself, wouldn't it have already been done? It was time to stand up and battle this Beast! I gathered as much strength as I could, but before I could get to both feet; the Beast bent over and put his face close to mine.

"What if you take off your Supermom Cape, and she..." I slammed my hand over his mouth before he could speak the unthinkable.

"**Nine**." The count was getting close.

It was time to change my focus. I wanted to step back onto the planet that had been spinning without me. I attempted to get on my feet when the Beast made his move. His sharp claws closed around my throat. The Beast is strong, and I was getting weaker with every attempt to free myself from his grip.

The referee was about to call the final number when I heard a chorus of voices yell,

"Stand up!"

Part II:

Putting Back the Pieces After All Hell Breaks Loose

You can put the pieces of your life back together, heal your broken heart, and find joy and happiness. You can learn to live in peace (most of the time) and find your confidence.

I discovered there are nine critical actions in a successful battle with a Beast. These are the Actions, that when taken independently and collectively can help you put back the pieces of your life after all hell breaks loose.

When our lives have been turned upside down, we tend to search for that one magic action; one quick jab that will send our Beast flying, but there is no magic bullet. Nobody is going to come along and sprinkle magic fairy dust over you. It is your right and responsibility to stand up and battle your Beast.

Each of these actions can be worked independently from the others; however, each Action works in conjunction with the others. When all nine are working together, the results are incredible.

The order of importance or success may be different for each person. Decide to Stand Up and Fight was purposely placed first in the order. It may not seem as important as some of the other Actions, but without first making a decision, none of the other Actions can be taken.

The Nine Actions to Battle Your Beast

1. **Decide to Stand Up and Fight** (I mean really decide, don't just say it).

2. **Get On Your Spiritual Armor** (In a battle with a Beast, you need to call in the big Gun!)

3. **Put On Your Oxygen Mask** (Give yourself permission to really live.)

4. **Build Your Circle of Strength** (Don't step onto the battlefield alone.)

5. **Change Your Attitude** (This is a battle changer.)

6. **Adjust Your Focus** (What we focus on becomes magnified.)

7. **Stop Being a Control Freak** (Focus on things that you can control.)

8. **Stand <u>On</u> Your Story** (Whatever you have done or been through - become better, not in spite of it, but <u>because</u> of it.)

9. **Make Meaning From the Madness** (Your story matters. Your experience, wisdom, strength, and courage can make a difference in the lives of others.)

Whatever Beast you have been living with, be comforted in the knowledge that you're not alone. Odds are thousands, or millions of others are familiar with your Beast. Yours has unique characteristics because your life story is unique, but many people are traveling, or have traveled a similar road.

For much of the time I was living with my Beast, I felt very alone. When I stood up to fight, I learned just how many people are fighting a similar battle.

When you stand up, there may be some people who are important to you who may not be as supportive as you would have assumed. It seems impossible the people you love the most will not be your biggest supporters, but it may happen. Some may even prefer you get back down on the mat. Don't pay any attention to them; don't be discouraged by them.

The world cheers for people who fight. Stories of those who have battled to overcome injustice, illness, heartbreak, bad decisions, addictions, and so much more, inspire us. We may be fascinated by the lives of people who seem to have it all. We root for the people who have been down on the mat and found a way to stand up and battle their Beast. Theirs are the stories that empower us; that make us believe we too can fight and win.

When you have won the battle, the people you expected to be standing with you may not be there. You may be bloodied and scarred from the battle, but you will be standing, and you will not be alone. When you look to your right, and you look to your left, there will be a row of people standing shoulder to shoulder with you. Some of them will be people you don't even know today. Be encouraged. The right people will show up at the right time.

What matters right now is that you have the power to change your life. The decision is yours.

Your Beast

I use "the Beast" in describing our challenges as a way to separate a situation or stronghold, from who we truly are. Your Beast wants to keep you from joy, happiness, courage, and hope; anything and everything that is positive. That is your Beast, but that is not who you are. You are far more than the Beast that is living with you.

You know if you are living with a Beast. It may simply be that you don't know what to do about it. You cover your eyes and stick your fingers in your ears, and chant, "La, la, la, la, la." You pretend you don't see the Beast in the room, no matter how many times you run smack into him.

A Beast attacks you in four ways. An attack on one of these will affect the other three.

1. Emotionally

When you are living with a Beast, the emotional roller coaster will leave you drained and vacant. Your Beast will work you over until you're heartbroken, sad, depressed, worried, disappointed, confused, overwhelmed, frustrated, and angry - all at the same time.

When you're emotionally drained for an extended period, mental paralysis is around the corner. You may begin to experience health issues. Your spirit begins to wither and your faith along with it.

2. Mentally

You spend countless hours agonizing over what you could have done differently. If your Beast is attached to another person's, you waste mental energy trying to think your way through their problem, one that you have no control over. You cannot stop thinking about your problem, your Beast, another person, or the other person's Beast.

Your Beast will keep your mental focus on things that are counterproductive to improving your situation and your life. He will keep you confused and unable to make decisions. Mental paralysis paves the way for unhealthy decisions, contributing to your already compromised emotional, physical, and spiritual well-being.

3. Physically

If your Beast can drain your physical energy, he can keep you from thinking clearly. Physically drained, you will be less able to nurture your spirit or to take care of your emotional well-being.

If the Beast has his way, your health will be compromised, ensuring you will have less energy to fight.

4. Spiritually

The Beast will attack your spirit, distract you from a connection with God, and help to destroy your faith. He cannot afford for you to call in your "Big Gun," so he will do whatever he can to keep you from spiritual peace, maturity, and wisdom.

The Beast is on a mission to destroy your energy, faith, happiness, health, hope, joy, peace, perspective, purpose, relationships, self-confidence, and strength. My Beast nearly completed his mission. Don't let yours win.

Helen's Beast

Helen's Beast was multi-faceted. Her husband passed away a few years ago, and she was heartbroken and lost. It had been years since Helen had worked, and she couldn't get herself to create a new resume', let alone get dressed up for a job interview. She was depressed, lonely, and scared, and was still angry at Jared for leaving her alone to raise Seth.

Her son was struggling to find his place in high school. Helen would fluctuate between encouraging Seth and flying off the handle at him for no reason. His grades were slipping, and he quit soccer, a sport he had played since he was a small boy. He stayed in his room most of the time or went out without telling Helen where he was going or where he had been.

Helen was worried about Seth but too preoccupied with her own emotional state to focus on her son. When she did interact with Seth, often she would blow up for no reason. Although she apologized later, her explosive behavior was affecting her relationship with Seth and negatively affecting her self-esteem. She felt like a terrible mother and a failure, in general.

Helen finally recognized her Beast and began to take action.

Acknowledging the Beast

Deep down, you realize you're not living the life you were meant to live. Your Beast has you focused on the past, fearful of the future, and unable to live fully in the present.

If you have been living with a Beast for some time, you're beyond tired. The world seems to be turning without you. You are fearful and anxious. Your dreams have all but died. Your self-esteem or self-worth is in the toilet.

It is time to recognize your Beast. You know what it is, and what it's doing to your life. Your Beast is standing right in front of you. It is understandable if he seems larger than life, and you're scared. Therefore, you walk around him, pretending not to notice. Living with this Beast has become your way of life.

I beat a path around my Beast for years, believing Jordan was the only one with living with a one. I refused to recognize my Beast.

Don't be concerned that you don't have all of the answers right now. You will figure this out along the way. Your Beast will not be taken down in one move, so don't be concerned that your energy is drained. It's a process, and you will develop the energy, courage, and stamina that it takes to battle your Beast.

Waiting on Someone Else to Change

Often, our life struggle is as a result of somebody else's actions or behavior. We are waiting for them to act or to change, and then our situation will change, as a result.

Belinda worked while her husband attended medical school. She helped to build and manage Ed's medical practice. In recent years, Belinda stopped working at the practice and focused on raising their three boys.

Ed earned a significant income, and they lived in a beautiful home and took lavish vacations. To the onlooker, it appeared that Belinda had it made. She didn't complain, after all she had everything she had ever dreamed of having, and Ed worked hard.

The flipside to Ed's success was that in his free time, he golfed, played basketball, or watched sports with his friends, rather than attending his boys' activities, or spending time with Belinda.

Ed insisted on hosting parties, sometimes both Friday and Saturday nights on the same weekend. Belinda spent hours planning, preparing and playing the good hostess. Although she didn't drink much, the booze was always flowing. Invariably, Belinda would clean up and go to bed while Ed and his buddies continued well into the morning. Belinda reasoned this was Ed's way of relaxing after a difficult week caring for patients, and performing surgery.

As the years wore on, she began to wear out. Belinda sat Ed down one Sunday afternoon and voiced her concern about his drinking and his absence in the boys' lives. She didn't bother to address how unhappy she was.

Ed went ballistic. He paced the floor, yelling at Belinda. He accused her of being ungrateful and spoiled. Women would line up to have her lifestyle. If his partying were such a problem, he asked her to explain how it was that he had built and ran a very successful medical practice while she stayed home doing nothing.

Belinda didn't like confrontation and wound up apologizing to Ed. He left the house and returned very late that night. She told the kids he had been called to the hospital on an emergency. It wasn't the first time she had lied to them in order to cover for Ed, and it would not be the last.

Belinda was incredibly unhappy, but rather than deal with her pain, she poured her energy into the boys and their lives. Her dream of opening a small boutique was out of the question. She was too busy ushering kids from one event to the next, and making sure the household ran perfectly.

Belinda gained some weight over the years, making her feel unattractive. It didn't help that Ed was so intoxicated most nights, that he had no interest in sex. She often wondered if he was having an affair, but was afraid to ask. Ed belittled her in front of friends. His friends laughed. Their wives laughed. Belinda laughed too but only on the outside.

Slowly Belinda was losing herself. She clung to her children, and when they grew older, the only thing Belinda had to talk about was the boys. She could barely stand the sight of Ed, yet she was scared to death that once the boys were out of the house, he would leave her.

Belinda reasoned year after year that once the practice reached a certain level, Ed would be under less stress, and he would return to the Ed she had married. She told herself that if she kept the house perfect and the kids out of his hair, he would be happy again.

Belinda began dressing provocatively, in an attempt to get Ed to see her, but he didn't seem to notice. His friends did; she saw their looks and heard the whispers.

Belinda was waiting on someone else to change before she began to change. The problem was Ed didn't recognize his own Beast. If Belinda chooses to wait for Ed to recognize his Beast, she will probably be waiting the rest of her life.

Comparing Your Beast

We compare things. It allows us to gain perspective on a situation, person, or problem. Be careful when it comes to comparing Beasts. It is not a competition.

You will run into people whose situations don't seem to be as challenging as yours. There will be others who make you feel as if your story pales in comparison to theirs.

Comparing your Beast to another person's Beast is dangerous. If yours appears to be smaller, you will have a tendency to underestimate your situation. It may cause you to minimize your pain and, therefore, to not seek help. When your Beast seems larger than another Beast, you might become insensitive to what another person is going through.

Your Beast is yours alone, and your journey is yours to travel. There will always be another person with a Beast that looms larger than yours. There will always be smaller Beasts. It is best to stay away from the measuring stick when it comes to a Beast.

It is time to gear up for the battle.

Action #1: Decide To Stand Up and Fight

"When you're knocked down, stand back up and keep battling. Your Beast can knock you down as many times as he likes. You just have to get up one more time than you are knocked down. Stay in the ring until the final round."

— *Valerie Silveira*

We take hundreds of small actions every day, and major ones less frequently. Actions such as taking a shower don't take a great deal of conscious thought while a life changing decision such as a career or marriage might take months of thought. Whether it's a simple or a major decision, all actions are preceded by thoughts. Before you take an action, you make a decision.

Some of the most important decisions we can make, those that can change our lives for the better, are the most difficult to make. Real change takes work, and most people either don't want to change or don't want to go through the uncomfortable process of change.

How many times have you made a New Year's Resolution that didn't last through January? In order for your life to change for the better, you will need to take serious and consistent action. Before any action can be taken, you must first make a decision.

You are reading this book because there is something that is holding you back from being happy, at peace, or living with hope. You are feeling helpless or heartbroken. You live with shame and guilt. You are angry, resentful, frustrated, and confused. You want to have a better attitude and focus on the right things, but you're obsessed with someone or something. You are mentally, emotionally, physically, and spiritually drained. You may be living in paralyzing fear or waiting for someone to change so your life can change.

If you can relate to one or many of these thoughts and emotions, it is time for you to make a decision. I felt as if this "thing" had control over me and I was clueless as to how to battle it. As a drug addict, my daughter is living with a Beast. As a Codependent Enabler, I too was living with a Beast. They come in many forms, and only you know what kind of Beast is living with you. Only you can make the decision to stand up and fight.

Pivotal Decision

Decide the time is now, and you're worth whatever it takes to get there. Decide you're *all in*, and you will stay in the battle no matter how long it takes, or how challenging it becomes.

You have probably tried taking action before, and possibly, you are taking some action now. When you finally decide you're going to stand up no matter how many times you are knocked down, it will be a pivotal decision.

Once I made my decision and began to use the very actions in this book on a daily basis, everything in my life began to change - fast. I will not tell you it has been smooth sailing, but at least I finally had a roadmap. Over the years, I had wandered around attempting to employ pieces and parts of each Action. It wasn't until I got them all working to some degree simultaneously, that I began to realize massive change.

There were many factors involved in my decision. One major factor was the realization that I have zero control over Jordan and whether or not she will ever battle her Beast, let alone beat it. I had to face the harsh reality that in my lifetime, I might not see Jordan take control of her Beast.

I was standing at a crossroads, beaten down and not sure which way to turn. Up ahead in the road that I was already on was more of the same. The other choice was to take whatever energy I had left and head down the other road - the one that led to freedom from my Beast.

There I stood staring down the road of despair, the road I knew all too well. I looked over at the road to freedom and saw roadblocks, mountains, and monsters. I knew it would be a challenge, but I was done with the other road.

It was my choice; nobody was going to make it for me. Before I took a step forward, I hesitated. It felt as if I was leaving Jordan behind on that road of despair. Truthfully, Jordan had already left me. Therefore, I made a decision - it was time to take my life back. That is just what I did.

You too are standing at a crossroads. It is time for you to take your life back.

Stand Up

My son, Sean played many different sports, most of them team sports. As a parent, the most nerve-wracking sport to watch was wrestling. Although wrestling is an individual sport, it's also a team sport. Sean was in the heavyweight division, and it was always the final match, and sometimes the deciding match, to see which team would win. The spotlight was on the lone mat and two heavyweight wrestlers.

At tournaments, in the early elimination matches, several mats were laid out with multiple matches going on at the same time. Family and friends were allowed to stand by the mats during those early matches.

Rich and I stood at the mat during once such tournament. This particular match pitted Sean against a very strong and more experienced opponent. Sean started the round in the down position, on all fours. His opponent had a tight hold on him as

Sean struggled to get up. He was on his feet, but unable to fully stand up.

His coach paced nervously while the two boys struggled; Sean to free himself, and his opponent to take him down to the mat. As he paced, the coach yelled until he was red in the face,

"Stand up Sean! Stand up!"

I had visions of Sean's back going out if he tried any harder to stand up with a very heavy guy on him. I was about to say something to the coach, when Rich gently grabbed my arm. Eventually, despite his opponent's efforts to drop him to the mat, Sean stood up and ultimately won the match. His coach knew he didn't stand much of a chance unless Sean found a way to stand up.

My Beast had me down on the mat; I was heartbroken, terrified, and exhausted. My Codependent Enabler Beast was strong, and I was becoming emotionally, spiritually, and mentally weaker by the day. My decision to stand up quite possibly saved my life.

You may be down on the mat, with your Beast on top of you. If you don't stand up, you too will be pinned. Just as Sean's coach yelled at him, I'm yelling at you (in love),

"Stand up!"

Decide to Stand up and Fight.

The World Keeps Turning

So far, Jordan has spent her late teens and her twenties in the belly of her Beast, detached from her family. She missed nearly every Christmas and Thanksgiving, and all birthdays, including her own. There was an empty seat at family dinners and a hole in my heart at family gatherings.

Jordan's Beast caused her to miss the weddings of three cousins, and the birth of one of their babies. She missed the memorial services of her aunt and her beloved grandfather.

Her drug Beast kept her from the family that could support her recovery. Sadly, my Beast kept me from enjoying much of those same years, and made sure I felt like an outsider, even when surrounded by people who love me.

 Has your Beast kept you from participating in your life?

We get one time around. Each second that passes is gone forever, never to be retrieved. You can make more money, get more stuff, and even create new relationships, but you can't make more time, no matter how brilliant, capable, rich, or wise you are.

When you are down, the world is not going to stop turning. It is your responsibility to find a way to get back up.

Precious Time

When you allow a Beast to continue to consume you, essentially you are giving away your precious time. Consider how much time you have already spent feeling as if the world is spinning without you; all of the time you can never recover.

Imagine for a moment that when you were born, you knew the exact number of days you would live. How would you choose to spend your allotted time? When you were younger, it seemed as if you had nothing but time left. The older we get, time seems to move more quickly, but, of course, time keeps moving at the same speed it has always moved. It is simply the closer we get to the inevitable; we begin to recognize the value of precious time. The saying goes: "time flies when you're having fun." I disagree - time flies whether you're having fun or not.

With time seemingly moving faster, how much more time are you willing to spend before you decide enough is enough?

The *"Why"* in the Road

Humans want to know how things work, and why they are the way they are. Those questions have led to advancements in technology, science, medicine, and psychology. When life throws you a curveball, you will ask *why* in a way you have never asked before. It moves far beyond curiosity, to a desperate need to understand why this is happening to you.

When Jordan's Beast grabbed a hold of her, I began to ask *why?* Why me? Why my daughter? Why my family? Why did Jordan become a drug addict? Why was she drawn out of her beautiful, wonderful, safe, happy life and into this dark place? Why won't she stop? Why did she have to be shot? Why can't I make her stop using drugs? Why am I the only one feeling this way right now? Why is everybody else enjoying their lives? Why me?

Finally, I asked myself this: Why *not* me?

Consider the possibility that your obstacle, pain, or heartbreak could be a catalyst for good. The very thing that nearly took you down could be the situation that propels you to a place you never imagined. The Beast you lived with for so long could be the very thing that gives you a unique perspective of the lives of others. What has occurred may not be fair, but since it's a reality, why not take your pain and decide to find meaning in the madness?

 Why not you? Why not be the person who overcomes?

If You Can't Do It For Yourself

Making the decision to stand up and fight will require energy, commitment, stamina, a good attitude, and much more. It may seem as if you don't have the courage right now to take the first step, let alone put all of the pieces of your broken life back together.

In a sense, I had accepted a *life sentence.* I had come to believe my best days were behind me, and it was not possible for me to be happy again until Jordan beat her Beast. I was defeated, and although I stood at the crossroads, knowing I needed to choose life, I wasn't sure I could do it - for myself.

I found the courage to stand initially because of, and for, my son. He had been through enough - losing his first friend and his only sibling to the drug addiction Beast, and then slowly losing his mother. It pained me to think that one day Sean would be forced to describe his mom as a sad, lonely woman. I didn't want to miss an opportunity to show Sean that even in your darkest hour, it's possible to stand up and fight. At the time, I found it much easier to fight for someone else's sake than my own.

Remember Belinda? She put up with Ed's verbal abuse and neglect "for the kids." Belinda finally realized that allowing her sons to grow up watching their father belittle and verbally abuse her, was hurting them. The boys were learning to be selfish with their time and disrespectful, in general. If they emulated their dad, they would treat their wives and children the same.

Belinda had allowed her self-esteem to become so low, that she found it hard to take a stand on her behalf. Ultimately, she decided to stand up and fight, for the good of her children. She insisted Ed go to counseling with her, and to address his drinking problem. Ed resented the demands Belinda placed on him, didn't own up to the emotional abuse, and refused to acknowledge that his drinking was a problem. Eventually, Belinda divorced Ed. Her boys were supportive and admitted they never understood why she put up with their father's behavior.

Today Belinda is at peace and has gained much of her self-worth back. She is on the road to happiness, joy, and new relationships. At first, Belinda took a stand for the sake of her boys; today she fights for herself.

Initially I stood up to fight, mainly because of Sean. When I was knocked down again, I stood up because my husband deserved to get back the woman he married. Each time I stood up to my Beast, I gained a little bit more of my self-worth back, and today I stand because I'm worth it.

You have been beaten down, and might feel as I did, that it's easier to stay down on the mat than to find the last shred of self-worth or confidence you might have left. One way or another, it's time for you to get back up off the mat; to stand up and fight. If at first you cannot do it for yourself, do it for someone you love. Just do it.

 If at first you can't do it for yourself, who can you stand up and fight for?

Fight as if Your Life Depends on It

Nobody ever said life was going to be easy. Life can be sad, painful, and heartbreaking. I could have never imagined my brilliant daughter would wind up being shot by a gang member or addicted to drugs. My future looked bright at the time all hell broke loose. Your Beast may have been blindsided you.

I have asked Jordan why she doesn't stand up and battle her Beast. Her answer is that it is harder than I realize. I am sure a drug addiction Beast is hard to battle. I witnessed Jordan detoxing a few times, and it was horrible. I've read grim statistics on heroin addiction recovery, which are enough to make me roll into a ball and cry.

Jordan's path to *life* must seem nearly insurmountable. However, staying in her addiction will mean death, so her only real option is to fight as if her life depends on it because it does.

My Beast sucked the very life out of me and had me down on the mat with his claws around my throat. I was beginning to exist, rather than to live.

Have you lost your joy, hope, peace, self-confidence, and your sense of value? Are you obsessed with your Beast or somebody or with something that is causing you anguish and heartbreak? Is your life out of focus? Are you missing out on meaningful relationships, afraid to give or receive love? Are you pretending to be happy when you don't feel happy? Do you feel as if you're not really living?

There is a big difference between the noun, living, and the adjective, *living*!

 Fight this battle as if your life depends on it because it does.

Stay in the Ring Until the Final Round

" Never, never, never give up."
— *Winston Churchill*

Anytime you're making a life change; there will be setbacks. Some days it will feel as if you take a step forward, only to take a step back. On other days, you will take one-step forward and two steps back. Eventually, you will begin to take two steps forward and only one-step back.

As with any positive, life-changing endeavor, when you begin to take action, the forces of darkness will work to derail you. The harder you fight your Beast, the harder he will fight back.

There will be days when you are knocked down - it's inevitable. Don't become discouraged when that happens, just stand back up, dust yourself off, and keep battling. Your Beast can knock you down as many times as he likes, but as long as you get up more times than you are knocked down, eventually you will prevail.

 Stay in the ring until the final round.

Your Declaration

Complete the blanks in the Declaration. Read it aloud every day for as long as it takes for you to be *all in*.

<u>Decide to Stand Up & Fight Declaration</u>

I, _____ am in a

battle with a Beast. My Beast is: _____

_____

_____.

Today, _____, 20____, I will Stand Up

and Battle my Beast. I know that I will be knocked down,

but I declare that I will get up every time, and that I will

take my life back no matter how long it takes, or how

difficult the Battle may become. I am worth it.

Fitting the Pieces Together

The Nine Actions to Battle Your Beast can be focused on independently, yet each one is dependent upon the others. With all of the Actions working together, you will begin to put the pieces back together after all hell has broken loose.

Your decision to stand up and fight is critical to the process of putting the pieces of your life back together. Without a serious decision, you will probably quit when the going gets tough. Each time you meet with a challenge, remember you made a decision to battle your Beast, no matter how long it takes or how hard the battle becomes.

Changing old habits and behaviors takes time. When heartbreak is a part of your battle, it is more challenging. Ask yourself how challenging it has been to live with the Beast! Taking control will empower you, and little by little, you will gain the strength, courage, and wisdom you need to take your Beast down.

When you **Decide to Stand Up and Fight**, you are making the decision to work on the other eight Actions:

 Get On Your Spiritual Armor

 Put On Your Oxygen Mask

 Build Your Circle of Strength

 Change Your Attitude

 Adjust Your Focus

 Stop Being a Control Freak

 Stand <u>On</u> Your Story

 Make Meaning From the Madness

As you work through the Actions, you might find yourself becoming discouraged or derailed. When that happens, go back to the Declaration and read it aloud. You may need to re-decide from time to time.

Battle Reminders

Decide to Stand up and Fight.

Decide you will be the person who overcomes.

Remember that time is precious.

If at first you cannot do it for yourself, fight because of someone else.

Fight this battle as if your life depends on it because it does.

Stay in the ring until the final round.

Action #2: Get On Your Spiritual Armor

"Therefore put on every piece of God's armor so you will
be able to resist the enemy in the time of evil. Then after
the battle you will still be standing firm."

(Ephesians 6:13)

Standing Alone at the End

As much as we desire to trust in others, there can be a fear of being let down or duped. At some point in your life, somebody has been untruthful, taken advantage of you, or made a fool of you. Once you experience mistrust, it leaves you skeptical.

That same fear can hold us back from having faith in a higher power. What if you believe something that turns out not to be true? Worse yet, what will people think if you have certain spiritual beliefs that differ from theirs?

The last thing you should concern yourself with is what others think. When your time is up, wherever you go, you will be standing there alone. Your friends, family or coworkers will not be there pointing at you and laughing because you got it wrong. Why are we so concerned with what other people think of our spiritual beliefs? Your spiritual connection is between you and your God. In the end, it will only matter to **you** if you got it right.

We will move forward with the assumption that good and evil exist. You can choose to refer to these spiritual forces in whatever way makes you most comfortable. I am going to use God as our higher power, our maker, our collective spiritual source of energy and all that is good. Satan represents the opposite of God, and the source of all evil. However, I have given Satan a nickname - he is the Big Beast.

God@heaven. com

It is challenging for most people to discern the voice of God. I don't know about you, but I often find it confusing to figure out if I am hearing from God, or from me.

I have never heard God speak out loud, but it sure would be nice to hear a whisper, or better yet, to receive an email. His address could be: god@heaven.com. He is God so it would take less than a nanosecond for him to shoot off a quick message.

Since God is not contacting us via email, we are left to do our best to understand and communicate with God. We pray, meditate, go to church, study the Bible and learn from other people.

The point is not how we get to a relationship with God, but that we do.

Body, Mind, and Spirit

You are made up of body, mind, and spirit, but how much time do you really commit to nurturing your spirit?

Our bodies get a lot of attention. We go to the gym, wear makeup, go to the hair salon, and fill our closets with clothing. Some people go to the extent of having cosmetic surgery. We are inundated with the latest fad diets. Every other day, another study comes out about which foods are good for us, and which are not and each one contradicts the last. We feed, clothe, moisturize, satisfy, tighten, lift, energize, medicate and rest, our bodies. We are obsessed with our bodies in one way or another.

We hunger for knowledge and gladly feed that hunger. The brain processes a constant stream of information and stimuli. In today's technologically advanced world of instant information, our brains are bombarded, nonstop.

Often it's our spirit we ignore. When your heart is aching, you may try to think your way through the minefield.

If your situation lasts over an extended period, you might even be mad at God. I'm not afraid to admit that I have been mad at, disappointed in, and frustrated with God. The problem with getting to that point is your spiritual strength is critical to your battle and helps to support your mental and emotional strength.

Your spirit is your heart and soul. Don't put it in last place.

Beasts Are Tough, But God Is Tougher

If there is a school of Beasts, you can bet the Big Beast is the headmaster. Never underestimate the power of the Big Beast, and, therefore, the power of your Beast. Keep the armor of God on at all times.

My Beast beat me up physically. In more than ten years, I had no more than a handful of restful night's sleep. I was an emotional wreck. Mentally, I was drained; trying to understand what was happening and attempting to figure out what to do about it.

In the darkest days of my journey, I couldn't put two thoughts together and was on the verge of tears every moment, and I was physically exhausted. During these times, it was my connection with God that gave me the strength to keep going.

It is what will allow you to keep going when you think you can't take another step. Beasts are tough, but God is tougher. God is your *Big Gun* in the battle with your Beast.

Faith Over Fear

Faith is never more tested than when you are on the Roller Coaster From Hell, riding in the dark with a Beast, terrified of what is around the next corner.

An acronym for fear is:

False

Evidence

Appearing

Real

Most of what we end up worrying about never happens. Fear keeps us alert to danger, but excess fear can be paralyzing. Fear is exhausting on every level.

It takes more energy to live in fear than to step out in faith.

"Only when we are no longer afraid do we
begin to live."
— Dorothy Thompson, Journalist

I have a fear of heights. Standing at the edge of a cliff, or next to a window in a skyscraper makes me physically ill. I highly doubt you will ever catch me jumping out of an airplane or bungee jumping.

Many years ago, I decided to conquer my fear of heights. I went in a hot air balloon and flew in a small airplane from Scottsdale to the Grand Canyon.

I went hiking to the top of Mt. Pilchuck and stood out on a rock outside of the lookout building. I had hiked the same mountain before and bravely climbed the ladder to the lookout, but had to climb right back down to solid ground. This time I walked around the outside deck of the tiny lookout and stepped through a break in the railing and onto a plank leading to the rock in this photo.

Fear isn't always rational. Clearly, there is little chance I will fall out of the window of a skyscraper, yet it still scares me. Many people are terrified of air travel. Statistically, there is a far greater chance of dying in a car on the way to the airport than in an airplane crash. However, people who have a fear of flying continue to hop in their car every day without giving it a thought, and still require a tranquilizer before boarding an airplane.

Fear is the opposite of faith, and it's not from God; it's one of the battle tactics the Big Beast uses to separate you from God. The more you give in to your fears, the more control the Beast has over you.

To the contrary, fear backs down when you face it. The Beast backs down when you stand up to him. When you're wearing your spiritual armor, the Beast shudders.

Face those fears! Recognize you're scared, but stand strong in the face of fear. The more you stand up to your fears, the less fearful you will be.

Although there is no guarantee that when you live in faith, your battle will be easier, just imagine what condition you would be in without faith.

What do you fear most? Is your fear rational? Consider how you can move from fear to faith.

The Big Social Security Office in the Sky

It is natural to feel blessed when life is going your way. There were times during my battle where I thought I would scream if I heard another person with a big bank account or thriving adult children say, "I'm just blessed."

Giving heaven the big "thumbs up" is second nature, when your bank account is full, the bills are paid, your job is going well, everyone is healthy, the kids are flourishing, your marriage is still in the honeymoon stage, and friends are aplenty.

There is a tendency to thank God when everything is going our way and to wonder why God is punishing us when our world is falling apart. Try staying in faith when the #@$&*! hits the fan.

When all hell broke loose for me, I dropped to my knees a number of times begging God to step in and take away the pain. The truth is I wanted him to change the situation; I wanted him to make Jordan change. When he didn't, I was upset with God. I wondered why other people got to be "blessed" and not me.

In my darkest days, I wondered if God had me mixed up with someone else; with someone who could handle all of this. You may be wondering the same thing.

I jokingly looked to heaven and slowly read the digits of my social security number, stating there had to be a snafu in the big social security office in the sky. They clearly had me mixed up with someone who could handle the pain of a drug-addicted child, financial challenges, health issues...one trial after another.

It turned out God wasn't mixed up. He knew what was around the corner, and just how much I could handle.

Stand strong wearing your spiritual armor, and you will discover you have much more courage and strength than you ever thought possible.

Faith When You're Not Feeling It

When Jordan went off the rails, and I couldn't get her back on track, my faith was tested. My faith wavered as Jordan lay in a hospital bed with a bullet in her abdomen, and I stood in the hallway yelling at God. The realization that she was a heroin addict and that I was powerless to stop her no matter how many times I prayed caused my faith to be shaken.

My faith has been tested, just as yours has. I will not mislead you into thinking I have had some superhuman faith through it all. To be truthful, I kept seeking God simply because I didn't know what else to do.

Faith When the Teacher Is Silent

"These trials will show that your faith is genuine.
It is being tested as fire tests and purifies gold."

(1 Peter 1:7)

The turning point in your faith might well happen when you feel as if you have nothing left. There have been extended periods of time where I couldn't hear from or feel God's presence at all; nothing, zip, zilch. These situations caused me a tremendous amount of confusion, distress, and fear. I am not a very "religious" person, and I am not super comfortable being demonstrative when I go to church, but alone I dropped to the floor many times begging to hear from God.

It seemed that at times the more I sought God, the quieter he became. I cried out to him like a mad woman, but the silence continued. I tried to figure out what I was doing wrong and why

God wouldn't show himself to me when I was trying so hard to find him.

I learned the teacher is often silent while the student is taking a test. In those times when you feel far from God, do not panic, it may be only a test.

Patience

We all have our strengths. Unfortunately, we all have weaknesses; one of mine is patience, and it has caused me unnecessary stress over the years. Impatience creates frustration, intolerance and a great deal of disappointment. I had always admired people who had an abundance of patience.

Right around the time all hell broke loose, I got down on my knees, and boldly asked God for patience, and then I got back up and waited. To this day, I'm not exactly sure what I was waiting for, but I must have assumed I would simply start being patient. After all, before I put in my request, I did admit my weakness, apologized, and asked for forgiveness. What more could I do?

It seemed as if I had no sooner asked for patience when all hell broke loose. Upon hearing my request, God didn't thing, "I know how to force Valerie to become patient; I will allow her only daughter to take up with a gang member and survive a near-fatal gunshot wound, only to become an addict. I will make sure she goes through a lot of pain and heartbreak. Yep, that should help her develop patience."

No, that is not how it went, but in his infinite wisdom, God knew what the future would hold for Jordan, and he used it to help me to develop more patience.

I will never be the most patient person in the world, it's not in my DNA, but I'm a hundred times more patient than I was the day I put in my petition. My prayer was answered, but not in the way I had expected.

I hope I didn't scare you off from asking for patience. It is not developed overnight, and without pain, but it's worth it. You will have to do your part to develop patience, and it has a great deal to do with faith.

 Be bold enough to pray for patience.

The Frantic Quest For Peace

Frantic is not exactly the word that comes to mind when one thinks of peace, but it helps to illustrate just how important it is to strive for peace.

Too often, the level of peace we experience is in direct proportion to how well things are going in our lives. Hardship, heartbreak, disappointment, and troubles will hit all people to varying degrees. They are unavoidable; a part of the deal that comes with living on planet earth. The key is to come to a place where you can find peace during times of trouble.

The world may tell you that you have no right to feel peace in the midst of your storm - don't listen to the world. The Big Beast will try to convince you that as a parent, you cannot possibly be at peace when your child is headed for disaster - don't listen to the Big Beast. Your Beast will reason with you that you can't afford to be peaceful, that you need to stay on high alert - turn away from your Beast. You have every right to be at peace, even in the eye of the storm. God offers you the gift of peace that surpasses all understanding. Unfortunately, most of us are not good receivers of this gift.

I came to the realization that life with a drug addict could mean that the storm would never cease. That reality helped spark my frantic quest for peace. If I had no control over the circumstances, then I needed to gain control over how I reacted to them.

Finding this kind of peace will require you to give up control and to put your faith and trust in God, in hopes that peace will help you to weather the storm.

When all hell breaks loose, your natural tendency will be to attempt to control the situation. I have *given it to God* many times, only to begin giving him pointers. It's like saying,

"I know you've got this God, but here are some bullet points, just in case."

My frantic quest for peace has turned out to be pretty miraculous considering the control freak I had become. I am not at a place where I'm sitting on an island, my feet in the sand and a smile on my face while the sharks swarm around me, as depicted in this image. I still feel a raindrop or two and every now, and again the clouds darken my heart, but I'm getting there. I hope you do too.

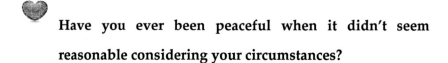

Have you ever been peaceful when it didn't seem reasonable considering your circumstances?

Does it make sense to strive for peace, even while your storm is raging?

How might you begin to find that type of peace?

Stop Looking For Your Crystal Ball

We want answers; we demand them. One of the questions that will play again in your mind is, "When will all of this be over?"

For three years, I kept wondering what Jordan would have to experience in order for things to change, for her to return to the Jordan she was before all hell broke loose.

When Jordan was shot, I thought for certain things couldn't get worse. That was in 2004, and things got a hell of a lot worse after the shooting. I spent the better part of the next decade asking the same question, "When will all of this be over?"

The reality is nobody knows the answer to that question. You may be in a similar situation where there is no *end* in sight, hoping for even a momentary glimpse into the future. Who has never wished they knew what their future held? The mystery of tomorrow has captivated people since the beginning of time.

There are those who have the gift of intuition, who are fairly good at predicting certain future events, but most of that is based on current realities. Nobody this side of heaven can predict the future with any degree of certainty, yet people keep trying.

Billions of dollars are spent each year on psychics, in the U. S. alone[iii] by people desperate to understand the future. It is an industry that shows growth during economic downturns.[iv] Our quest for knowledge and control leads us to believe that somehow if we know what is coming we can be better prepared, or able to alter the course of events.

We can modify our behavior, or make decisions that can impact future events, but there is no possible way to predict the future. There are too many moving parts for which we have no control. Every day we come into contact with other people, whose actions, motives, and decisions have nothing to do with us. Your life is filled with actions and situations you cannot control.

If you have a loved one who is participating in self-destructive behavior, there is continuous anxiety over the future. Your loved one has repeatedly been *lost*. If you're experiencing a serious health issue, you will want to know if and when you will be healed. You may have struggled to find a lasting relationship, or have been hurt and wonder when you will find true happiness with another person. Beasts can keep us in a constant state of panic and anxiety over the future.

Today is the only day you are guaranteed, so today should be the most important day of your life. We need to quit trying to figure out what is going to happen in the future. Instead, live in faith that you can handle whatever the future holds. Develop more peace, patience, and wisdom so you will be more prepared for the future, and able to live fully in the present.

 Stop searching for a crystal ball; you will never find one.

Thank You Very Much

It is easy to be thankful when everything is going well. How thankful do you feel when all hell breaks loose? That is when your faith is put to the test. It is when you begin to understand that not all blessings come in the form of big bank accounts, great jobs, loving spouses, or perfect children.

There is always something for which to be thankful. Start with the fact you are breathing. Every day you are given the gift of life you should hit your knees and thank God. If you can't find something to be thankful for right now this very moment, then you're not looking very hard.

 Stop right now and name something you're thankful for, and give God thanks for whatever came to your mind.

Several times throughout each day, recognize your gifts and blessings and be grateful no matter how small they may seem at the time.

Some of the most valuable blessings will come to you in the form of a roadblock, hurdle, or challenge, or in the form of a Beast. When all hell breaks loose, it can force you to your knees, or flat onto your face. The opportunity for spiritual growth is tremendous during times of trial. However, you may have to look harder to find it when your world seems to be falling apart.

When you can be thankful, not just in spite of your circumstances, but because of them, you will be far more thankful when things are going well.

Blessings and Miracles

*"The secret to happiness is to count
your blessings while others are adding
up their troubles."*

— *William Penn*

Jordan's bullet was lodged in her abdominal wall. The Guy pled guilty on a Wednesday, and on Sunday, Jordan called me and said the bullet had come out of her body. I knew this defied logic, considering the location of the bullet. She said she had passed it during a bowel movement.

I had only been *outside* of the apartment where Jordan was living. It was in a small suburban town not exactly known for violence, but the building wasn't in a particularly nice part of that town. After she had been shot, I continued to fear something else could happen to her. I jumped to the conclusion the bullet she found in the toilet could not be hers, but that she was living in a place where bullets appeared in toilets!

Jordan insisted, "Mom, it's not a different bullet. It just came out when I went to the bathroom."

I called our doctor and explained the situation to him.

He said, "It's not possible. The bullet is lodged in her abdominal wall. There is no migration path between the bullet and the digestive tract. It would have to make a hole in her colon, in order for it to pass in her stool."

The doctor ordered an x-ray to prove the bullet was still there. Nobody was more surprised than he was to learn the bullet we had brought to his office was indeed the 9-mm bullet fired from

The Guy's gun. He went on to explain that there was no medical explanation for this reality. He suggested we take the x-ray to the surgeon at Harborview, certain it would be written up in the medical journals as a medical miracle.

Have you ever prayed for a miracle? I have many times. We somehow have the notion that a big blessing comes with a big bang. It would be pretty cool if we were praying for a miracle, and suddenly a bolt of lightning came out of the sky, and a choir of angels began to sing. There were many times I secretly hoped God would grab me by the back of the shirt and pick me up off my knees.

Blessings are often subtle, and if you are not paying attention, you might miss the kindness of a stranger, or the perfect words spoken by a friend at the precise moment you needed to hear them.

Since they can happen slowly over time, you are often left with the impression that the turn of events wasn't a miracle, but rather came as a result of luck or your actions.

When I was on my frantic quest for peace, my prayer wasn't answered immediately. One day, though, I realized that I felt different. Afraid to believe I had somehow received the blessing of peace, I discounted the feeling. Day after day, in spite of the circumstances, I began to feel more peaceful. In fact, the situation with Jordan had spiraled further downward, yet I remained more peaceful than I had in years. The miracle of peace allowed me to start finding myself again.

 Blessings and miracles do happen, but you have to notice them.

Fitting the Pieces Together

When you **Get On Your Spiritual Armor**, you will gain more strength than you will find on your own, or from other people. It just might be your Spiritual Armor that gives you the courage to **Decide to Stand Up and Fight.** When you are wearing your Spiritual Armor, you're far more equipped to **Change Your Attitude, Adjust Your Focus,** and **Stop Being a Control Freak.** Your faith will help you to forgive yourself and allow you to **Stand <u>On</u> Your Story**, rather than in it, and to **Make Meaning**

From the Madness that is your story. Spiritual strength reminds you of the amazing gift of people and the necessity to **Build Your Circle of Strength**. It will help you give yourself permission to matter and to **Put On Your Oxygen Mask**.

Battle Reminders

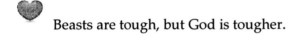 Beasts are tough, but God is tougher.

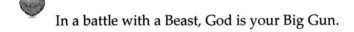 In a battle with a Beast, God is your Big Gun.

 Choose Faith Over Fear.

Develop patience.

Go on a "frantic" Quest for Peace.

Stop looking for a crystal ball; nobody this side of heaven knows the future.

Don't miss your blessings and miracles.

Action # 3: Put On Your Oxygen Mask

"Find out who is wearing your Oxygen Mask

and get it back."

— *Valerie Silveira*

The mechanic told my husband, "Your front brakes need to be replaced right now." Not good news, considering front brakes alone cost nearly $700. Needless to say, we had no choice. We had to replace the front brakes, and he told us the back brakes would be needed a few months later.

It is inevitable when you own a car that you have to maintain it. If you don't take care of your car, it's not going to last very long. Sometimes we treat our cars better than we treat ourselves. You can get another car, but there is only one YOU.

Too often, we take care of everyone else, and everything else before we take the time to care for our needs. Women are especially prone to taking a backseat in life. Mothers are cursed when it comes to even considering their needs before their children, husbands, friends, and even the family dog! When you're having trouble putting yourself at the top, at least get your name on the list.

Taking Care of You

Stress

In 1992, during a routine physical, my doctor noticed a lump on one of my thyroid glands. After several biopsies, the specialists were fairly certain it was a benign tumor. My doctor was insistent that I have it removed, in case a part of the tumor that had not been biopsied was, in fact, cancerous. I asked him what the odds were that the tumor was benign.

He guesstimated an 85% chance. If I were a gambling woman, I might throw down all of my money at a poker table in Vegas on an 85% chance of winning. I liked my odds so I decided to pass on having my throat cut open, telling him I would "leave it in there until it was a grapefruit hanging off my neck."

A year or so later, I was seeing a new doctor. After blood test results, she asked me,

"Did you know you have a thyroid disease?"

The tumor had not become a grapefruit, so it had slipped my mind when I completed the new patient paperwork. Shortly after that, I began to have symptoms of hyperthyroidism; I had an overactive thyroid.

For a period it was great; I could eat anything I wanted and was losing weight. Unfortunately, my heart had begun to race, and then my hands began to tremble. Had my new weight loss program not come with serious warnings, I would have been thanking the tumor.

Reluctantly, I agreed to drink radioactive iodine out of a lead container. In the nuclear medicine department, they shut me alone in a room with a heavy door, and instructed me to drink the liquid that would taste like stale water. The tumor in my thyroid gland was considered a hot nodule, meaning it was the overactive part of the thyroid.

The theory was that the radioactive material attached to the iodine would slip down my throat, into my bloodstream, and eventually into to my thyroid glands. It would destroy the hot nodule, and not the inactive parts of my thyroid, and without causing any side effects to my body. I walked out of the lead room, and my arm didn't fall off; I didn't grow a third eye, so I figured I was good to go.

Shortly after, I started to come down with frequent colds and bronchitis that would last for weeks. A couple of years later, after a quick ten-pound weight gain, and crawling up the stairs to my bed each day, I had another blood test. I was now hypothyroid; my thyroid was underactive, more like not functioning. Much to my disappointment, I would be on thyroid medication for life, and strapped with a condition that affected my metabolism. Among other things, this would mean a negative impact on my weight and energy level.

For years, my weight and energy level were only slightly affected by my thyroid condition. After several years on the Roller Coaster From Hell, it changed. My brain became foggy, and I never felt rested, no matter how much sleep I managed to get. I began to gain weight no matter how I ate, or how much I exercised.

A few years ago, I was working with an internist who specializes in integrative medicine and age management. After extensive blood tests, the doctor sat with me to go over the results.

"Your adrenals are shot," she told me.

Nobody wants to hear from a medical professional that anything is "shot." I understood the basics of adrenal glands but had no idea how this condition would impact my life.

"Have you been through an extended period of stress?"

I believe I may have laughed when she asked that question. I gave her a snapshot of the past few years. She nodded her head as if to say, "yes, that would do it."

Adrenal glands are located on the top of each kidney and are responsible for releasing different hormones. One of the many important functions of these hormones is controlling the "fight or flight" response to stress. No doubt, I had lived in a near-constant state of "fight or flight" for years.

I have always been a morning person; the kind of a morning person, that can irritate non-morning people. Never once have I pressed a snooze button on an alarm clock. While others were dragging themselves to the kitchen for coffee, I was bouncing around ready to go, and caffeine free. Now, it is all I can do to drag myself out of bed each day. My sleep became interrupted throughout the night and no matter how many hours I managed to accumulate, I would wake up as if I hadn't slept at all.

Currently, I am dealing with some other health issues. There is no question living with a Beast has physically beaten me up. Eventually, your Beast will beat you up physically.

Go Outside and Play

Nature is a great healer. There is nothing like the solitude of an early morning walk where there is no sound but the birds, or the breeze through the trees. Few things rival a mountain hike or a walk along a beach. Nature is an amazing setting to de-stress, think, or connect with your spirit.

A Time article in 2009 discussed "Eco-Therapy for Environmental Depression."[v]

> *"Depressed people often need someone to hug. On occasion, that someone may just be a tree. A new and growing group of psychologists believe that many of our modern-day mental problems, including depression, stress and anxiety, can be traced in part to society's increasing alienation from nature. The solution? Get outside and enjoy it. "*

Get into the outdoors. Spend time at a river, a lake, or at the ocean. Take a walk in the forest, or hike up a mountain trail. Take an early morning or evening walk around your neighborhood.

Go hug a tree.

Go outside and play!

Work It, Baby, Work It!

My trips to the gym began in high school. It was how my friend Janet and I justified downing a plate of tortilla chips smothered in cheese afterward. In those days, I could have skipped the workout since plates of nachos didn't impact my weight one way or another. Since my metabolism button was turned off, I can't even look at a plate of chips piled with cheese without gaining weight. I'm extra motivated to exercise due to the metabolism issues.

You might not be too excited about exercising, but the benefits are worth it, and not so that you can eat a plate of nachos. Aside from the fitness benefit, it also helps to decrease stress and increase energy.

According to WebMD.com, people who regularly exercise benefit with a positive boost in mood and lower rates of depression:

What Are the Psychological Benefits of Exercise With Depression? [vi]

Improved self-esteem is a key psychological benefit of regular physical activity. When you exercise, your body releases chemicals called endorphins. These endorphins interact with the receptors in your brain that reduce your perception of pain.

Endorphins also trigger a positive feeling in the body, similar to that of morphine. For example, the feeling that follows a run or workout is often described as "euphoric." That feeling, known as a "runner's high," can be accompanied by a positive and energizing outlook on life.

Endorphins act as analgesics, which mean they diminish the perception of pain. They also act as sedatives. They are manufactured in your brain, spinal cord, and many other parts of your body and are released in response to brain chemicals called neurotransmitters. The neuron receptors endorphins bind to are the same ones that bind some pain medicines. However, unlike with morphine, the activation of these receptors by the body's endorphins does not lead to addiction or dependence.

- *Regular exercise has been proven to:*
    - *Reduce stress*
    - *Ward off anxiety and feelings of depression*
    - *Boost self-esteem*
    - *Improve sleep*
- *Exercise also has these added health benefits:*
    - *It strengthens your heart.*
    - *It increases energy levels.*
    - *It lowers blood pressure.*
    - *It improves muscle tone and strength.*
    - *It strengthens and builds bones.*
    - *It helps reduce body fat.*
    - *It makes you look fit and healthy.*

Is Exercise a Treatment for Clinical Depression?

Research has shown that exercise is an effective but often underused treatment for mild to moderate depression.

Not only is exercise good for your physical health, but the endorphins released act as your natural happy pill!

If you're suffering from clinical depression, you should seek the advice of a professional.

Don't ignore the physical, emotional, and psychological benefits of exercise.

 If you're not regularly exercising, get going right away.

When the Sun Goes Down

My cat stays on the bed at night, but he doesn't sleep much. Shiska waits for the slightest movement as an indication that it's time for the three of us to get up. He goes through periods where he doesn't bother waiting; instead, he sits next to the bed and meows just loud enough to wake me.

Like Shiska, the Beast is wide-awake at night, waiting for any chance to wake you from a restful sleep. He takes the opportunity the darkness of night provides, to increase your fear. When you are awake in the night, your already overstressed brain may go into overdrive, making it nearly impossible to fall back to sleep. You will toss and turn, unable to shut down your thoughts.

If sleep does come, when you awake, you feel no more rested than when you went to bed. This continuous cycle, and your body's inability to rejuvenate will make it harder for you to see the light at the end of the tunnel.

Sleep is critical for healing and energizing the body, mind, and soul. There are numerous methods people use successfully to get a good night's sleep. Some of them are:

- Prayer
- Meditation
- Yoga
- Hot bath
- Tea
- Warm milk
- Hot shower
- Essential oils
- Removing all electronic devices from the bedroom
- Sleep mask
- Sound machine
- Earplugs

- Counting sheep (that didn't work for me; I once counted to five thousand!)
- Sleep medication

Work to find something you can do to get a good night's sleep. If a lack of sleep has become a serious problem, you may want to consider seeking medical attention.

Laughter is the Best Medicine

Not many people would argue the benefits of laughter, but did you know studies have proven the psychological, mental, and even physical benefits of laughter?

The Mayo Clinic published an article stating that a good laugh has more benefits than lightening your load mentally. They explained that laughing actually induces physical changes in your body and can: stimulate many organs, activate and relieve stress response, sooth tension, improve your immune system, relieve pain, increase personal satisfaction, and improve your mood. [vii]

The sitcom, "Seinfeld" that ran from 1989 to 1998, and is still shown in syndication is a great example of *everyday life humor*. It was referred to as "a show about nothing," but in reality, it was a show about everything. Each episode dealt with a subject or several subjects that were relatable. It allowed us to laugh at the characters, and at ourselves. Finding the humor in everyday life, will lighten the load you're carrying. We need to be more serious about not being so serious.

 Do you try to find humor in everyday life?

One morning, years ago, I stood in a circle chatting with a few coworkers before the workday began. The Wonder Bra, with its small removable bra pads, had hit the United States.

As I talked with my coworkers, I noticed one of my bra pads had escaped and was lying on the floor near my foot. Glancing around the circle, it appeared nobody else had noticed, so I carefully slid my foot over and stepped on the bra pad.

As the conversation began to wind down, it would have been natural for me to excuse myself and head to my office, but I stood frozen unable to move without revealing my secret. I waited awkwardly until the last person walked away, before bending down and scooping up the bra pad. I retreated to my office, closed the door, and laughed my head off. Of course, I couldn't wait to retell the story.

Can you recall a time (or two) when you started to laugh and couldn't stop? What adolescent or teenager has not laughed in class; unable to stop, even after being glared at by the teacher. Okay, maybe that was just me.

Have you ever laughed when it seemed inappropriate? When my grandfather died, my mother and I were at the funeral home, wrapping up the preparations for the memorial service. The funeral director was finishing some paperwork and suggested we go take a look at the chapel where the service would be held.

His directions led us down a long hallway, lined with doors. We were in conversation and not paying much attention to the doors. As we passed one of them, we couldn't help but notice a woman standing over a body. My mom was startled and let out a gasp, causing the woman to look up from the body as we passed by the open door.

The situation seemed very funny to me, but I didn't want to offend the woman as I was uncertain as to whether or not she was a family member or simply worked at the funeral home.

Stifling my laughter, I took off at a dead run toward the chapel, with mom following. We burst through the doors and fell onto a pew, laughing hysterically. No doubt, my Scottish grandfather with his whacky sense of humor was lying across his pew in heaven, laughing with us.

We should laugh every chance we get. If you're not prone to laughter, get around some funny people or watch a funny television show or a comedic movie. Find the humor in everyday life. As long as you're not laughing at other people, do whatever it is that makes you laugh; it's a free prescription for good mental and physical health.

Codependency and You

Codependency is a common word in the world of alcohol or drug addiction. The term was originally used to describe people who were in a relationship with a chemically dependent person.

Once again, I refer to a certain definition of codependency: "A codependent person is one who has let another person's behavior affect him or her, and who is obsessed with controlling that person's behavior."[viii]

The term codependency wasn't new to me, having heard it used over the years in reference mainly to spouses of alcoholics. I didn't pay much attention to the term I would one-day use in describing myself.

For me, it happened gradually, and by the time I realized what was happening, I was living as a codependent. In looking through definitions and lists of behaviors, I can see now that I have a tendency toward certain codependent behaviors. It's natural for me to put the interests or well-being of others before my own. Had Jordan not become addicted to drugs though, I might not have recognized myself as having a "mild case" of codependency.

A young woman in recovery said to me recently, "You're the worst kind of person to be the mother of an addict since you are so generous and put others first. An addict will eat you alive."

It can be uncomfortable for some of us to admit, even to ourselves, that we have codependent tendencies, or that we are demonstrating serious codependent behavior. The codependency label didn't sit very well with me since it flies in the face of my independent and confident nature, but when Jordan went sideways, my codependent tendencies surfaced.

If the actions and behaviors of your loved one are causing you to lose your identity or to obsess over that person's life, you are in danger. Codependency is like a thief, robbing you of your perspective, independence, and self-love. Had I not found a way to manage my codependency, I was in danger of completely losing me, and anyone else I cared about.

 Are you in danger of losing yourself in the actions and behaviors of another person?

Who Is Wearing Your Oxygen Mask?

If you have traveled by air more than a handful of times, you pay very little attention to the flight attendants as they go through the pre-flight safety demonstration. Next time you're on an airplane and the flight attendants begin the process, look around at the other passengers, and see what they are doing. You will see people talking, reading, staring out the window, or already in dreamland. Now and then, you may notice a passenger or two listening and watching intently as the flight attendant goes through the drill; they are probably infrequent air travelers. Those of us who have been on hundreds of flights could recite the pre-flight instructions in our sleep.

One important part of the demonstration is the explanation of the oxygen mask. We are told in the case of a loss in cabin pressure; an oxygen mask will be released from the overhead compartment. Instructions are given as to how to properly place the oxygen mask on your face and exactly how the mask will react as you begin to breath.

You are further instructed to **put the oxygen mask on your own face before trying to assist others around you.** If you pass out, you will not be able to help anyone around you. **Who Is Wearing Your Oxygen Mask?** Think carefully about this.

Yes, we should give some of our oxygen to others. Sure, we should allow them to lean on us from time to time, but be careful you are not focusing most of your energy on another person, at the expense of your own well-being. Living with a Beast is tiring; attempting to control how another person behaves or compensating for their behavior is beyond exhausting. When your oxygen mask is on somebody else's face eventually, you are going to pass out.

 Figure out who is wearing *your* Oxygen Mask and get it back. Then put it on your own face and breathe.

Is It Okay For You to Be Okay?

Guilt Trip

I love traveling; meeting new people and experiencing different cultures and customs. There is one trip I have taken extensively - the guilt trip. You may have taken a few of these trips yourself.

If your Beast is tied to another person's behavior, then you struggle with whether or not it's okay for you to be okay when your loved one isn't.

As the mother of an addict, I lived with the constant guilt over enjoying life while my daughter was poisoning her body. It didn't feel right for me to feel peaceful while Jordan was lost. I would begin to enjoy myself, only to allow an overwhelming feeling of guilt to wash over me, ruining the moment or the entire day. As a mother, how was I to leave my only daughter behind while I moved on with my life?

Stepping Over

Annette's first marriage was to a man who was a raging alcoholic. He became infuriated when Annette paid bills with his drinking money. Although she loved him, Annette was at the end of her rope. She called Tom's mother and was surprised by her response.

"You need to step over him," Tom's mother told her.

She was a recovered alcoholic and knew firsthand that Tom was holding Annette back. It was the mother's *permission* that allowed Annette to *step over* Tom and move on with her life. Years later, Tom called Annette to make amends.

It was the mother's choice of words that likely saved Annette from many more years of anguish. She didn't suggest Annette leave Tom or walk away from him. She told Annette to "step over him." In other words, it was Tom's choice to stay where he was, but Annette was not required to stay there, drowning with him. She could keep moving, stepping over him, on her way.

Tom's mother told Annette it was okay for her to be okay, even though her son wasn't. It was a selfless thing for a mother to do, and she was able to do it because she understood that only Tom could save Tom.

Just because someone else is choosing not to be okay, it is still okay for you to be okay. In fact, choose to be better than okay.

Give Yourself Permission to Matter

Others can try to convince you that you matter, but until you give yourself permission, nothing will change. Rich tried to get me to focus on myself over Jordan for years. Friends encouraged me to do the same. Certain family members voiced concern about my mental, physical, and emotional health. People who had walked the codependency path advised me that it was time for me to help myself. They all gave me permission to matter, but it wasn't until I gave myself permission, that I began to matter to me.

You may or may not have people in your life who encourage you to take care of yourself. If you're an approval seeker, your natural tendency will be to wait for the approval of others. In either case, you could be waiting awhile. Ultimately, you have to be both the permission giver and the permission receiver.

Logically, Jordan is the last person from whom I should need permission to take care of myself. For some reason, there was a long period when I was waiting for permission from her. The drug Beast is selfish and self-centered and would never have given me the permission.

Whether or not another person gives you permission or changes their behavior, you <u>must</u> give yourself permission to put the pieces of your life back together.

Fitting the Pieces Together

When you **Put On Your Oxygen Mask**, you will have more energy and stamina for battle. Giving yourself permission to matter will ensure that each time that you are knocked down, you will **Decide to Stand Up and Fight**, one more time. Self-love will give you more reason to **Change Your Attitude, Adjust Your Focus and** to **Stop Being a Control Freak.** Self-care inspires you to **Stand <u>On</u> Your Story.** Believing in yourself is essential for believing you can **Make Meaning From the Madness.** Loving yourself will allow you to love others and to **Build Your Circle of**

Strength. Realizing you matter to God will propel you to **Get On Your Spiritual Armor.**

You don't need permission from me or anyone else, but just in case it's the nudge you need: I hereby give you permission to matter. Now give it to yourself.

Battle Reminders

If you can't put yourself first, at least get your name on the list.

Go outside and play.

Create some natural happy pills by exercising.

Find a way to sleep.

Move past Codependency.

Get your Oxygen Mask back.

Give yourself permission to put the pieces of your life back together.

147

Action #4: Build Your Circle of Strength

"On those days when you don't have the strength to fight, let your Circle of Strength fight for you, then stand up again."

—Valerie Silveira

Don't Step Onto the Battlefield Alone

We all need someone to lean on, to love, to learn from, to lead, and to follow.

The more out of control Jordan's life became, the more I began to retreat. My comfort zone is being there for others; being strong at all times. While I clung to my so-called emotional strength, I was becoming weaker by the day. I preferred hiding in the walk-in closet crying, to being vulnerable enough to allow the people who care about me, to care for me.

You may have your Spiritual Armor strapped on, but you will still need your Circle of Strength. Don't step onto the battlefield alone.

The Circle of Strength

Although each journey is unique and personal, they are intertwined with the journeys of others. The Circle of Strength represents your people. There are four distinct groups in the Circle of Strength.

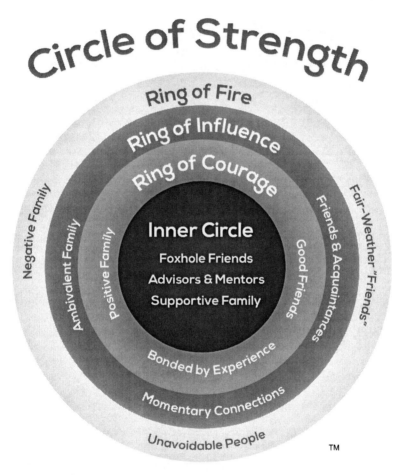

Circle of Strength

Ring of Fire

Ring of Influence

Ring of Courage

Inner Circle

Foxhole Friends

Advisors & Mentors

Supportive Family

Negative Family

Ambivalent Family

positive Family

Fair-Weather "Friends"

Friends & Acquaintances

Good Friends

Bonded by Experience

Momentary Connections

Unavoidable People

TM

Inner Circle

At the core of the Circle of Strength is the Inner Circle. This group of people includes your foxhole friends, trusted advisors and mentors, supportive family, and possibly your spouse or partner.

Ideally, you should spend the greatest amount of time with those people in your Inner Circle; however, circumstances may prevent you from doing so. Despite the amount of time you spend with the people in your Inner Circle, be certain you are greatly influenced by them. These are the relationships that will give you the most courage, strength, wisdom, knowledge, and comfort necessary for you to stand strong in your battle. These are the people that will battle with you.

Foxhole Friends

A foxhole is "a small pit, usually for one or two soldiers dug as a shelter in a battle area."[ix] A foxhole friend will be at your side during the battle; next to you in the foxhole, and on the battlefield with you. Not only would a foxhole friend fight alongside you, but they would be willing to go out onto the battlefield and drag you back into the foxhole. Much is asked of a foxhole friend so they will be few and far between, but worth their weight in gold.

If you don't have at least one foxhole friend, work on developing a relationship to the point of having one. The best way to gain a foxhole friend is to be one.

 Who is (are) your Foxhole Friend(s)?

Trusted Advisors and Mentors

You might automatically assume your Inner Circle will be comprised solely of your family and friends, but some of the most valuable people in your Inner Circle might be trusted advisors or mentors.

Often, we confide in spiritual leaders, counselors, life coaches, or mentors more than we do with others in our Inner Circle. You may feel more secure sharing your innermost feelings with one of these advisors or mentors, and can gain a perspective from them that others close to you are unable to provide.

 Do you have advisors, mentors, teachers, pastors, spiritual leaders, counselors, or life coaches in your Inner Circle?

Family Members Who Support You Unconditionally

The bond family members have with one another can be some of the strongest bonds imaginable, or the most challenging. Not all of your family members will be in the Inner Circle. Since we all crave the approval of our families, it can be devastating when those you were certain would be the most supportive, end up letting you down. I am not suggesting you start cutting ties with family members unless they are abusive or antagonistic. We simply need to have realistic expectations when it comes to family or anyone else.

During my darkest days, I received some strong support from a few of my family members. Hopefully, there will be members of your family who <u>are</u> a part of your Inner Circle, but it is not necessary to include everyone simply because they are your family by blood, or by marriage.

Spouse or Partner

It would stand to reason your spouse or partner would be part of your Inner Circle simply by virtue of your relationship. Based on what the Inner Circle represents, they may not fit. They may even be preventing you from standing up.

If your spouse or partner is not part of your Inner Circle, you need to determine why. I am certainly not advocating divorce or the ending of relationships. However, there are situations in which the very relationships that should make us better are destroying us. If that is the case, you should take a long hard look at your relationship, and take action to change the dynamics of that relationship. Life is short, and getting shorter every day.

 Is your spouse or partner in your Inner Circle? Why, or why not?

The right people in your Inner Circle will fight with you, and for you. On those days when you don't have the strength to fight, it is okay to lie down. Let your circle fight for you. Then stand up again.

 Who is in your Inner Circle?

Ring of Courage

The first ring surrounding the Inner Circle is the Ring of Courage. It is comprised of good friends, positive family members, and people who are bonded to you by a common experience.

Good Friends

Mom always said you could count your true friends on one hand. Those true friends are your foxhole friends that reside in your Inner Circle. Beyond your foxhole friends, and far greater in numbers than foxhole friends, are your good friends. You can share most of your thoughts and feelings with them. Good friends may not drag you off the battlefield, but they just might be in the foxhole with you. For sure, they will be there for you most of the time.

 Who are your good friends?

Positive Family

While a few of your family members may support you unconditionally, others will simply be a positive influence. They love you and will express genuine concern.

They are not in your Inner Circle, but the mere fact they are positive is incredibly valuable. Be thankful they are in your corner, cheering for you.

Bonded By Experience

Along the way, you will meet people who are on or have been on, a similar path as yours. With some of these people, you will develop an instantaneous bond.

As close as family and friends may be, most of them have not walked in your shoes. They may be empathetic, sympathetic, loving, and supportive, but unless they have been where you are, it is difficult for them to relate. A unique bond exists among those who have shared similar challenges and heartbreak.

There are many support groups people join for this very reason. The bond of life experience can be very strong. Find some people you can bond with over your common experience. A few may even end up in your Inner Circle.

Be careful, however, you don't wind up adding more stress to your battle. Many people have no real interest in battling their Beast. They have begun to identify themselves with their pain. We all know that misery loves company. Make sure people you bond with because of common experience are also standing up to their Beast, and not simply trying to suck you into living with theirs.

Ring of Influence

In your Ring of Influence are your friends and acquaintances, ambivalent or non-supportive family and people with whom you have momentary connections.

Friends and Acquaintances

Most of the people we refer to as "friends" may actually be acquaintances. Call them what you want, these relationships do have a positive influence on us and our battle. If nothing else, these types of friends can distract you from your troubles for an evening.

They don't know you as well as your good friends and may not ask much about your situation, which can often be a big relief. There were many occasions when I was down, and Rich drug me to a social event with friends or acquaintances, or to meet new people. Often I didn't want to go, and I made excuses not to attend once in a while. Most of the time, I went for Rich's sake, but every time came away thankful I had gone.

People in this group can be a source for new perspectives on your situation. Since they are not as intimate with your life or your battle, they are sometimes able to give insight that others closer to you are unable to provide.

You need an occasional break from your troubles, and even from the battle. People in your friends and acquaintances group can provide you with a much-needed distraction or break.

Ambivalent or Non-Supportive Family

Members of families can be the best of friends and the most supportive and encouraging. They can also be some of the most negative, unsupportive, ambivalent people you will come across.

There is a sense of obligation and duty to stand beside family, and, therefore, some of the so-called support we receive from family isn't genuine.

Don't assume they don't care, as people react to situations in different ways. It could be that you have always been strong and so they are not used to offering support, or perhaps they are unsure how to help or what to say. Some family members are simply selfish or self-absorbed.

It is also possible some of your ambivalent family members might be living with a Beast of their own. The world is full of all kinds of people, and so is your family.

Momentary Connections

Have you ever met someone and had an instant connection with them? Have you had a stranger say something that, to this day, you have never forgotten? Have you ever had an interaction with someone you have never seen again, yet every time you think about them, you feel happy or energized?

Momentary connections can help in unexpected ways. A kindness from a stranger can remind us of our humanity. One brief comment can stay with us for the rest of our lives. In turn, an opportunity to extend a hand, or give a word of encouragement to someone we don't know, allows us to rise above our circumstances.

So impactful are some of these brief encounters that I was tempted to include them in the Ring of Courage. Since they are chance encounters, they have been included in the Ring of Influence, but don't discount the importance of these moments. The next time you go shopping, out to dinner, or meet a stranger while on a walk, smile and say hello. Ask how the other person is doing. You never know when these momentary connection opportunities will present themselves.

Ring of Fire

I fell into a burning ring of fire,

I went down, down, down, and the flames went higher

And it burns, burns, burns, the ring of fire.

— *"Ring of Fire" by Johnny Cash*

The Ring of Fire in Your Circle of Strength is full of the people who are challenging to be in a relationship with. They might be a family member, an acquaintance, or a coworker. Typically, the people in your Ring of Fire are those people you can't easily avoid. If there are people in this group you can avoid, and are choosing not to, you may want to ask yourself why!

Fair-Weather "Friends"

A fair-weather friend is one who is supportive only when it is convenient and easy, or when it benefits them. If a person is your friend when everything is going well but is conveniently absent when you're going through a rough patch, an argument could be made that they are not a friend. Thus, a fair-weather friend could more appropriately be named, a fair-weather acquaintance.

These fair-weather people may be difficult for you to remove from your life. It might be your friend from childhood that you still feel bonded with due to your long history. Maybe she is your sister-in-law. Or it's the charismatic friend, that when you are with him, makes you forget he is selfish, until the next time he lets you down.

Fair-weather people may be hard to remove from your life, or you may not choose to do so. If a fair-weather friend is in your life by choice, then don't continue to be surprised by the inevitable disappointments you will experience. Be careful not to allow these relationships to influence your self-esteem or your sense of value as a friend. Take them for what they are worth.

 Do you have any fair-weathered friends?

Negative Family

Newsflash - not all family members will support you. It has been said that "familiarity breeds contempt." The more acquainted one becomes with another person, the more that person's shortcomings are known, resulting in a sense of disrespect. Who knows us better than our family? Our families should love us in spite of our shortcomings, but that is not always going to be the case.

Don't put too much pressure on your family. As with all of your relationships, you have a natural chemistry and bonding with people at different levels. It is the same way with your family. We choose our friends, but, for the most part, we don't choose our family.

There will invariably be people in your family that, given the choice, you would never have chosen. Typically, these people are negative, cynical, and offensive about most things. Worse yet, they may be looking for company.

Negative people are hard to deal with in general and can be more of a challenge when they are family. You might choose to love these family members, but for your sake, limit the amount of time you spend with them. Unfortunately, negativity can be more contagious than positivity.

 What is your strategy for not allowing negative family members to impact you?

Unavoidable People

There are certain people, other than family members who are unavoidable. Often a coworker can be as challenging, or more so than a negative family member. Many people spend more time with coworkers than nearly anyone else. Unless you're the boss, you don't get to choose your coworkers. If you have a coworker who rubs you the wrong way, or worse yet, is incredibly negative, you will need to dig down deep in order to not be impacted by them.

Unavoidable people may be a spouse or family member of a friend. They could be a customer or a member of a club where you belong. If there is nothing you can do to avoid the person, you're going to have to put up an invisible shield. Don't let their negativity stick to you; try to let it slide right off of you.

I hope you're not dealing with too many negative people. Do whatever you can to take these people in small doses.

The Ring of Fire Can Actually Help You

After all of the warnings and cautions about the Ring of Fire, there is a silver lining. For much of the time, it may feel like more of a rust lining. There are some good things that can come out of the relationships with people you're "stuck with" in the Ring of Fire if you're willing to consider them.

First, negative or cynical people are a mirror. If you don't like what you see when you look into the Ring of Fire, be careful, you don't see yourself in its reflection.

Another benefit of the Ring of Fire is that it allows (or forces) you to develop patience, empathy, and tolerance.

If you can't avoid the Ring of Fire, why not take the opportunity to learn and grow from the people in that ring. When you look back, you might attribute some of your most important growth to the Ring of Fire.

List the people who are in the different areas of your Circle of Strength. Build and strengthen those relationships the right relationships. Be open to the lessons that can be learned from the Ring of Fire.

Broken Heart Glue

If you're alive, you will undoubtedly suffer heartbreak. The very heart scars you think will take you down are those that will make you stronger. When muscles are overworked, the fibers are torn down. Through this process, the muscle fibers become scarred, leaving them stronger. In the same way, a broken heart will be left scarred, but once healed it will be stronger than ever.

Unhealed heartbreaks can keep us from ever deeply loving or trusting again. They can cause you to become bitter, cynical, and to lose hope.

Although there is no plastic surgeon for the heart, there is something better. It is called Broken Heart Glue, which is love. The first person who can help you to mend your broken heart is you. Without self-love, it will be more difficult for you to accept love from others. Love yourself enough to let others love you.

If you have a broken heart due to a loved one's Beast, there are no doubt, so many cracks in your heart that it's hard to tell where one starts, and another ends. If you have lost someone close to you, then you have a gaping wound. In any case, it will require many applications of Broken Heart Glue. Thankfully, there is a never-ending supply. Turn to your Circle of Strength; they are holding your tubes of Broken Heart Glue.

 Who is holding your Broken Heart Glue?

Fitting the Pieces Together

Don't step onto the battlefield alone; **Build Your Circle of Strength.** Ultimately, you need to **Decide to Stand Up and Fight**, for yourself, but it might be your Circle of Strength that inspires, nudges, or pushes you to make the decision. Your Circle of Strength will remind you when you need to **Change Your Attitude** or to **Adjust Your Focus**. Your Circle will believe in you when you find it hard to believe in yourself and stand with you as you **Stand <u>On</u> Your Story.** They will cheer you on as you **Make Meaning From the Madness.** Some of the people in your Circle of Strength will help you to **Put On Your Oxygen Mask** and to **Get On Your Spiritual Armor.** Others will simply raise their hand, reminding you they are there for you and you can let go and **Stop Being a Control Freak.**

Battle Reminders

♥ Don't step onto the battlefield alone.

♥ Rely on your Inner Circle.

♥ Have at least one foxhole friend.

♥ Be a foxhole friend to at least one person.

♥ There is a tremendous opportunity to learn and grow from your Ring of Fire.

♥ Use your Broken Heart Glue.

Action #5: Change Your Attitude

"Weakness of attitude becomes weakness of character."

—Albert Einstein

Attitude is a Battle Changer

There is nothing you can do to change what has happened in the past. There will be things that happen in the future, for which you have no control. There may be but one thing in life you can truly control - your attitude. We get to choose every single day, in every situation, in each moment, what our attitude will be. There have been plenty of times I didn't have the right attitude. Countless words have flown out of my mouth that I wished I could take back. A bad attitude will always lead to negative words and negative actions.

The right attitude will result in words of encouragement, hope, and inspiration. A positive attitude will lead you to take positive actions. Have you ever had a great attitude and regretted it afterward? I doubt it.

Whether negative or positive, your attitude has an influence on those around you. Do you want to influence others with negativity, self-pity, and cynicism? Or would you rather promote happiness and hope? You have the power to choose. Attitude is a battle changer.

Do you have a desire to take control of your attitude and believe you have the power to do so?

Logic of a Negative Thinker

My childhood was challenging. Gone was a very young mother's college dream, along with, for the most part, the father of her three children. It was during those early years, sitting by the window waiting for my dad that I gave myself the first of many lessons on negativity.

In those days, we only had play clothes and school clothes. When we were to go with our dad, we got into our school clothes and waited for him to arrive. I sat with my two brothers on the sofa, looking out the window. Many times, he didn't show up. On those occasions, we would get off the couch and into our pajamas. As a disappointed little girl, I plodded off to my room with the dwindling hope that next time would be different.

I was tired of being disappointed by my dad; by many things in my young life. I developed a mentality that helped me to avoid disappointment. My philosophy was that if I thought the worst, I would never be disappointed. If something good happened, I would consider it a bonus.

Not only did I begin to live by that negative thinking, but I shared it with anyone who would listen! It horrifies me now to considering the negativity I perpetuated with my negative thinking logic.

Negative thinking may help to avoid disappointment, but it sure is a waste of a lot of time in between. Consider the number of hours, days, weeks, months, or even years in between disappointments that you live in darkness, without hope. It's not worth it.

If you are in a negative mode, it should come as no surprise when one thing after the next seems to go south in your life. Or that you begin to attract negative people like flies at a picnic. On the contrary, when you *expect* the best, you may be surprised when *coincidentally* people and situations that are more positive come your way.

 Do you lean toward the logic of a negative thinker or a positive thinker?

Pity Party

It is easy to end up at a Pity Party. They have nonstop advertising, aggressive marketing, and huge welcoming committees. If there were actual buildings, they would have easy to find, well-lit entrances, and greeters at the doors. The minute you arrive at a Pity Party, you will feel welcome. Strangers only moments before will become long lost friends.

Pity Party goers are not solution finders; they are waiting for someone else to swoop in and fix their problems. Regular attendees at Pity Parties seem to be happy only when they are unhappy.

If you find yourself at a Pity Party, it's advisable to head for the nearest exit. Unfortunately, finding an exit from a Pity Party will prove challenging. In contrast to the warm welcome, few people will help you locate the exit door. The closer you get the more resistance you will have from the other attendees. If you do find one, it will be a small, unmarked door at the end of a maze. Once you locate the exit, run for the door, and don't look back. Better yet, decline the invitation.

As tough as it is to extricate yourself from a Pity Party, it will prove even more so to leave a party that you have hosted. Throwing your guests out once you have invited them is much more problematic than excusing yourself from another person's Pity Party. It is best to stay as far away from Pity Parties as you can.

Two Types of Victims

If you are a victim due to the actions of another person, or a situation you were not in control of, then you truly are a victim. There is nothing wrong with acknowledging you have been victimized and giving yourself permission to process the emotions that come along with being a victim. There may be medical, psychological, financial, and legal issues to wade through. Certainly, those things need to be handled.

Becoming a victim may not have been your fault, but continuing to live as one is your choice. No matter which of life's two-by-fours smacked you over the head, you can decide whether or not you will remain living as a victim.

There are two types of victims, the Poor Me Victim and the Victim in Disguise.

Poor Me Victim

Poor Me Victims constantly solicit sympathy either directly or indirectly. Some Poor Me Victims will make it clear they want and expect your pity. Others take a more passive-aggressive approach when it comes to eliciting sympathy. These people will act as if they don't want your sympathy, but drop continuous hints or make offhanded comments, in hopes you will pity them or come to their rescue.

Neither tactic works well in the long run for the Poor Me Victim. Initially, people will respond with sympathy, but eventually they will grow weary, especially if the Poor Me Victim is not trying to change their circumstances or their attitude. Over time, a Poor Me Victim will be left with only other Poor Me Victims, or with people who feel obligated to be in a relationship with them.

Victim in Disguise

The second type of victim is the Victim in Disguise. These victims are strong; the people others rely on for strength and support. Not used to being needy, the Victim in Disguise is skilled at masking their pain.

Victims in Disguise are terrified of being considered victims, so they wear a mask to hide the pain, and then go home and cry themselves to sleep. Unlike the Poor Me Victim, Victims in Disguise may believe they need little to no support, and then find it hurtful when nobody offers.

Victims in Disguise may even try to convince themselves they are not in a battle or have won it, when the truth is they have simply learned to exist with their Beast. I was a Victim in Disguise.

Neither victim is a healthy way to live. Whether a Poor Me Victim or a Victim in Disguise, it is time to conquer the Beast and step out of victimhood.

 Are you a Poor Me Victim or a Victim in Disguise?

Coulda, Shoulda, Woulda

When Jordan and Sean were young, I would tell them there are three people you really need to avoid: Coulda, Shoulda, and Woulda. It would have served me well to listen to my own advice. Living with my Beast for nearly 13 years, I developed a very close relationship with Coulda, Shoulda, and Woulda. So familiar were they to me that I named them.

Mea Coulda

Mea Coulda tells you what you could have done differently. She is the image you have conjured up in your mind of the stress-free life you could only dream of living. Mea Coulda has escaped pain and heartbreak, floating through life without a

178

care in the world. Mea has the life you *could* have had; if only you had been luckier.

Shirley Shoulda

Shirley Shoulda preys on shame and guilt. Unlike *your* hindsight, Shirley Shoulda's foresight is 20/20. Shirley Shoulda is a know it all, and never misses an opportunity to get what she wants. Shirley Shoulda makes you doubt and regret every decision you have made and every action you have taken, or not taken. Shirley Shoulda never lets you forget what you *should* have done differently.

I. Woulda

Everything I. Woulda touches turns to gold. I. Woulda represents every person you have ever stood in awe of, wondering what it takes to live without ever making a mistake.

I. Woulda would never make a bad financial decision. He would never be in an unhealthy relationship, depressed, betrayed, abandoned, or unloved. Certainly, he would never have a child who is an addict.

I. Woulda is a constant reminder that other people are living worry-free, successful, productive lives. You could have too, if only you *would* have made different decisions.

Quit Hanging Out With Them

Mea Coulda, Shirley Shoulda, and I. Woulda are obviously not real people. They are life-like examples of our self-talk. When life goes sideways, we spend a great deal of time considering what we could have, should have, or would have done differently. Mea Coulda, Shirley Shoulda, and I. Woulda will keep you trapped in the past, beating yourself up over every move you have made, or not made.

Visiting the past can be helpful in understanding how or why certain things have transpired, or why you have developed certain characteristics. It can help you to avoid making the same mistakes.

Continuous trips into the past, especially with Coulda, Shoulda, and Woulda will keep you stuck where you are.

You know you need to throw them out of your life, but you keep inviting them back. Each time Mea Coulda, Shirley Shoulda, or I. Woulda show up, show them the door. This line of thinking is self-destructive and is sure to gain you express entrance to a Pity Party.

 Have you been spending too much time with Mea Coulda, Shirley Shoulda, and I. Woulda?

You Can't Poop Right

I attended my first *motivational seminar* when I was around eleven-years-old. It was at my friend Chris's house at her kitchen table, and the speaker was her dad, Ron. I don't recall what precipitated the speech, but I was still in my negative thinking period, so I needed it.

"You need to get your attitude right. If you don't have the right attitude, you can't eat right, you can't sleep right, you can't poop right, you can't do anything right."

Of course, two eleven-year-old girls cracked up when he said you can't poop right. Our giggles didn't deter Ron; he was dead serious, and he was right. When you have a bad attitude, you don't eat right, you don't sleep right, and sometimes you can't even poop right.

Ron probably doesn't remember that day at the kitchen table more than 40 years ago, and if he did, he might be surprised to learn I have never forgotten my first *motivational speaker*.

Each of us has an opportunity every day to give words of encouragement to others. You too could have a lifelong impact on an eleven-year-old who desperately needs an attitude speech about not pooping right.

If You Spoke to Others the Way You Speak to Yourself

I attended a three-day women's golf camp at our club a few years back. One afternoon, a sports psychologist gave a talk to the group.

She said, "If you spoke to others the way you speak to yourself on the golf course, nobody would ever play golf with you."

The room fell silent, other than the sounds of women shifting in their seats. My guess is the guilty look on the faces of the other women mirrored my own expression.

Women golfers tend to be very complimentary and encouraging of one another, but not so with themselves. I have watched women beat themselves up like Dobby the House Elf in the Harry Potter stories. I was Dobby, flogging myself for years on the golf course, and in many other situations.

You should avoid negative people. However, it is a little more challenging to avoid a negative person, when that person is you.

We could apply the same psychology we learned at golf camp to other areas of our lives. If you spoke to others the way you too often speak to yourself, you wouldn't have many friends.

 Are you speaking to yourself the way you want others to speak to you?

 Try to go an entire day without talking negatively to yourself; it may be harder than you think.

It's Time to Fly Again

Years ago, I had a repeating dream that I could fly. No matter the scene, I would spread my arms and fly as if it were the most natural thing in the world. Even if I had been standing with another person, I always took to flight alone. I soared above the earth feeling courageous, peaceful, and free.

Each time I woke in the middle of a flying dream, I shut my eyes tight and laid still, begging my brain to take me back to the dream. Never able to get back, I waited in anticipation of another flying dream, never knowing if or when I would fly again.

After a few years, I stopped flying. It has been more than 20 years since I spread my wings and soared like an eagle.

When I was pushed onto my Roller Coaster From Hell with my Beast in control, another dream emerged. This time I was high school age and was at home when I realized I was supposed to be at school. I was in a panic because I remembered I was to take my finals but couldn't recall which classes I was in or what I had been studying. No matter how hard I tried, I couldn't figure it out.

In each dream, I raced to my high school, only to realize I had not been there in so long that I had no idea how to find my classes. I knew I had a locker assigned to me but had no idea where it was or if it contained my books. I rushed to the school office to get a copy of my schedule, only to discover a long line of students and the big hand on the clock telling me I had one minute to get to class.

My dreams tend to be very realistic, sometimes taking a few minutes or longer for me to shake the feeling the dream was real. School was fairly easy for me, and I never had a problem with grades, so on the surface it appeared strange for me to have a dream that I was struggling with high school. Of course, my recurring dream had nothing to do with high school; it was my mind trying to reconcile my tumultuous life. It was symbolic of my helplessness and frustration.

During the years that I had the magnificent flying dream, I was in a period of my life where I was confident and hopeful. I was on a great career path, finances were in order, and my children were happy and safe.

When I began to lose my daughter, I began to lose my self-confidence and my hope for the future. One of my children was no longer happy, or safe.

No doubt, you have been through periods in your life where you were *flying*. You may not have had the same repeating dream, but life was full of possibilities. Once all hell broke loose in your life, you were stuck, as I was stuck in my repeating high school dream.

When I got up off the mat and started to fight, I stopped having the high school dream. Unfortunately, I haven't had the flying dream again. Not yet. It is time to fly again.

It's time for you to fly again!

Ten Percent of My Life

A couple of years ago, I reconnected with some of my high school friends. We were having dinner, and I looked across the table at Christine when it occurred to me that I had never seen her with short hair. She always wore her thick, dark hair, long. I said across the table, "Christine, I've never seen you with short hair; you look great." The friend next to me elbowed me and whispered that Christine had battled cancer - twice. I turned red and apologized, telling Christine I wished I had known so I could have at least offered a word of encouragement.

Her reply is frozen in my mind.

"I purposely didn't tell a lot of people because I wanted this thing to take up about ten percent of my life."

She only wanted cancer to take up ten percent of her life! If you want to change your attitude, get around some people like Christine - the 10% of my life people. Better yet, work to be a 10% of my life person. You won't get there all at once, but it is a good goal to work toward.

If you had to put a percentage to your Beast, how much of your life does it consume?

Attitude, by Charles Swindoll

The longer I live, the more I realize the impact of attitude on life.

It is more important than the facts.

It is more important than the past,

than education, than money,

than circumstances, than failures, than successes,

than what other people think or say or do.

It is more important than appearance, giftedness or skill.

The remarkable thing is we have a choice

every day of our lives regarding the attitude

we embrace for that day.

We can't change our past.

We can't change the fact that people

will act in a certain way.

We can't change the inevitable.

The only thing we can do is play on the one string we have,

and that is our attitude.

I am convinced that life is ten percent what happens to me

and ninety percent, how I react to it.

And so it is with you.

We are in charge of our attitudes.

The Power of Attitude

There is something in your control that acts as a weapon, with the potential to affect countless people. In the hands of the wrong person, this weapon is a toxic contagion, infecting everyone it comes into contact with. It cannot be contained or locked in a vault to avoid infection. The only way to stop this noxious contagion is to alter it. The weapon is a negative attitude, and the only way to stop it is to change it.

Negativity doesn't take a great deal of effort; most people tend to lean toward negativity. If you want to stay in the negative attitude zone, you will have plenty of help. You need only to watch the news, read the paper, or talk with your neighbor. Truthfully, you don't have to turn on the television, pick up the paper, or leave the house. It may be as easy as listening to your own thoughts.

Within you is a powerful force, that when unleashed, is just as contagious as the negative attitude toxin. It is your positive attitude.

Forty years later, someone will talk about the time you said something that helped to build the foundation for their positive attitude, just as I refer to my friend Chris's dad, Ron.

You may not have the power to change every situation, but in all situations, you do have the power to choose your attitude. In a battle with a Beast, a positive attitude is a battle changer.

 Reflect on recent events and consider ways in which your attitude could have been more positive.

 Could your positive attitude have made those situations better?

Fitting the Pieces Together

As you work to **Change Your Attitude**, other areas of your life will change too. The right attitude will prompt you to **Decide to Stand Up and Fight**. The ability to **Get On Your Spiritual Armor** and to **Put On Your Oxygen Mask** will be greatly influenced by your attitude. The right attitude will allow you to **Build Your Circle of Strength** faster and stronger. Without a positive attitude, it will be nearly impossible to **Adjust Your Focus** or to **Stop Being a Control Freak**. Your attitude will influence your decision to

Stand <u>On</u> Your Story rather than in it and will push you to **Make Meaning From the Madness.**

Battle Reminders

A positive attitude is a battle changer.

Stay away from Pity Parties.

Are you a Poor Me Victim or a Victim in Disguise?

Stop inviting Mea <u>Coulda,</u> Shirley <u>Shoulda,</u> and I. <u>Woulda</u> over.

Talk nicer to yourself.

Get on board with the logic of a positive thinker.

Get around some "10% of my life" people.

Work to become a "10% of my life" person.

Spread your positive attitude virus around.

Action #6: Adjust Your Focus

An old Cherokee told his grandson,

"My son, there is a battle between two wolves

inside us all.

One is Evil. It is anger, jealousy, greed, resentment,

inferiority, lies, and ego.

The other is Good. It is joy, peace, love, hope,

humility, kindness, empathy, and truth."

The boy thought about it and asked,

"Grandfather, which wolf wins?"

The old man quietly replied, "The one you feed."

— Author Unknown

Keep Your Social Media Microscope in Focus

When all hell breaks loose, it's natural for your perspective to get out of focus. During your darkest days, it will appear everyone has what you have lost.

Social media has allowed us to connect with those we have lost contact with, and to stay in touch with friends and family. Thankfully, most people have chosen to post the happiest and most positive aspects of their lives on social media platforms, which have become go-to places for inspiration and motivation. However, let me issue you a warning:

> *"Lives Lived Out on Social Media*
>
> *May Appear Better Than They Really Are"*
>
> *— Valerie Silveira*

Although positive news is much better than the alternative, social media can leave us with a false sense of others' lives in comparison to ours.

What you focus on becomes magnified. When you experience loss, it's natural to become more aware of what others have. The more loss I felt as Jordan moved deeper into her addiction, the more it appeared every other mother had a perfect daughter.

To my aching heart, Facebook posts seemed to appear daily stating people had the "best daughter in the world." They went on to suggest I share the post if I too, had a daughter I was proud of, who meant the world to me, and so on. There were times when I didn't even know where my daughter was, or even if she were alive.

It wasn't just the "world's best daughter" posts, it was everything. It seemed as if the entire world had the best husband, drank the best wine, went on weekly dream vacations, swam with the dolphins, drove the coolest cars, had the best friends in the world and bulging bank accounts; perfect lives. The postings were not the problem. Clearly, I was out of focus.

Be careful not to spend too much time focused on momentary messages. Nobody has a perfect "anything." During a battle with a Beast, you will need to re-focus constantly in order to maintain perspective. Some people have what you don't, but it's counter-productive to focus on another person's journey. Most of them are not what they appear to be anyway.

Everybody Has a Story

If you are peering through the window of somebody else's life and it looks perfect, chances are they haven't cleaned their windows in a while. Other people's lives are not perfect in spite of how they may appear to you. The same darkness comes upon everybody at night. The same sun rises in the morning.

Everybody has challenges and struggles. We all know people whose lives are easier than ours, and I have no explanation for that, but it's useless to spend valuable time attempting to figure it out, and it doesn't matter.

When it appears what you're going through is far more challenging than others around you, it could be a timing issue. While you're feeling your way around in the dark, or battling a Beast, you're sure everyone else is on a beach sipping drinks with umbrellas in them. Life happens in cycles, and there will come a time when each person will have some type of challenge.

The more time you spend focused on another person, longing for their life, the more convinced you will become, that your life is never going to change. The gap between the imaginary perfect life others are enjoying, and yours, will continuously widen.

Before long, it will feel as if you are standing at the Grand Canyon. On one side, you stand with your troubles, with your Beast. Eighteen miles across, stand all of the other people who have somehow escaped life's misfortune. As you look longingly across the great expanse, straining to see the faces of those more fortunate, you will miss one simple fact - everybody has a story.

Standing there feeling alone, turn around and take a look beside you and behind you. As far as your eye can see, and beyond, will be those who have been where you are, or worse. Everybody has a story.

It's Time to Start a New Movie

Stephanie has a fear of abandonment from early childhood. Her father had all but abandoned her, leaving her mother to raise Stephanie and her brothers and sisters. She had a happy childhood, but Stephanie couldn't seem to get past her father's decision to leave, or the shame and anger she felt toward the addiction Beast he had yet to conquer.

Although not yet thirty, Stephanie longed to find a husband. She became hyper-focused on her married friends and became convinced she had a flaw, or many flaws that kept her from meeting her future husband. By all accounts, Stephanie is a beautiful person, yet she has low self-esteem.

Stephanie met Adam and was sure she had finally met *the one*. He had all of the qualities Stephanie had been looking for; she was sure of it because she had a list, and one by one, she placed a check mark next to each quality Adam possessed. He already had a successful career; he was handsome, drove an expensive sports car, owned a condominium overlooking the city, and had tons of friends. Everyone loved Adam, including Stephanie.

Things were going well for a few months, but then Adam started to be a bit distant. He forgot to call her, broke dates claiming he had to work late at the office and was remiss in returning her calls. Stephanie feared that Adam was going to leave her so she did everything she could to be better.

Each time *perfect* Adam let her down, Stephanie tried harder to look better; to act better. The more distant he became, the more Stephanie tried to change, and the more she tried to hang on to Adam.

Eventually, Stephanie's worst fear was realized when Adam broke up with her. Stephanie was devastated. She went over every detail of her relationship with Adam and agonized over what she could have done differently. The all too familiar feelings of abandonment from her father surfaced, and she became depressed.

Stephanie was out of focus in a couple of different ways. First, Adam wasn't perfect, and in fact had demonstrated he was not who she thought he was. Instead of recognizing that, Stephanie chose to blame herself for the breakup.

Next, Stephanie was relating a broken relationship with a guy to her feelings of abandonment as a result of her father. She was having a hard time understanding that everyone goes through breakups, and most people have been through several failed love relationships over their lifetime.

If Stephanie can find a way to recall the true events of the relationship with Adam and to separate her feelings of abandonment with her father, from other relationships, she will begin to stare down her Beast.

Stephanie has a choice which movies she wants to run in her mind. She can continue to replay the breakup and abandonment movies, or she can choose to replay movies reminding her of all the people who have stood by her; far more than the one who abandoned her.

We have to be very careful we don't keep playing the same movie and expect a different ending. Sometimes it is time to pop in a new movie.

 Have you been playing a movie (or movies) you know you need to change?

Cycle of Hope and Massive Disappointment

Disappointment is the result of unmet expectations. In healthy relationships, it's reasonable to have certain expectations. In a marriage, for example, we should expect our spouse to be faithful.

Our children are expected to follow the rules at home and school. It isn't wrong to expect certain things from personal relationships.

Disappointment occurs when we place unrealistic expectations on others. It is reasonable to trust your child in your home. If that child is a drug addict who has stolen from you in the past, then it would be unrealistic for you to expect different behavior while they are using. In Stephanie's case, it would be unrealistic for her to expect her father to be there for her when he hasn't been since Stephanie was a young girl.

Each time you place unrealistic expectations on another person, it will invariably be followed by disappointment. We should continue to expect certain behaviors or levels of trust in our relationships, but we need to manage those expectations.

When someone shows you by their actions, who they are, believe them. People can and do change, but until they demonstrate otherwise, be careful placing expectations that you know in your heart will set you up for massive disappointment.

Managing disappointment and trying to live with hope can be a bit of a balancing act. Having a daughter for an addict keeps me constantly walking the tightrope, in an attempt to balance the two. For years, I lived in a constant cycle of hope and massive disappointment. I never want to lose hope that one day Jordan will finally tame her Beast. If my hopes are too high, they will likely be followed by massive disappointment.

The statistics for an addict beating heroin are very low. Understanding the statistics, I still hope, pray, and encourage Jordan to be one of the few that beat it. Still, I need to manage my hope and expectations with the reality of the situation.

You too need to manage expectations. You should strive to have a positive and hopeful attitude, while avoiding the highs and devastating lows, particularly if your Beast is a related to another person's Beast.

The hope and disappointment grid is an example of some of the highs and lows I have experienced and demonstrates movement toward more of a balance between hope and disappointment.

The idea is to avoid extreme highs followed by devastating lows. You will fall into the disappointment zone at times. The goal is to find your way back into the hope zone.

CYCLE OF HOPE AND DISAPPOINTMENT

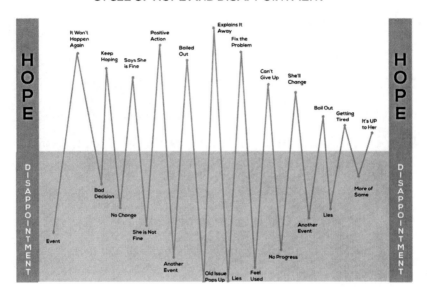

Isolation

The longer Jordan was lost, the more I began to retreat. I wore out the movie of the life I *should have* had with my daughter, and each time I did, the more heartbroken I became. It was increasingly more difficult to hide my emotions; to pretend I was fine. It became easier to isolate myself.

When offered an invitation to meet new people or to socialize with friends, I did everything I could to decline. I had a list of excuses but didn't want to disappoint Rich, so I only used them when I was too exhausted to pretend. If not for my husband, I may have opted out of all social engagements.

In a situation of ongoing grief, you feel very alone, regardless of the number of loving people around you. For a time, I didn't know anyone with a child who is an addict, so I felt very isolated.

This story that illustrates what I was allowing to happen to me; possibly, what you are allowing to happen to you:

The Old Woman in the Cave

Victoria was walking down the street one day when she stopped at a wide hole in the ground. Years before she had noticed a small crack in the same spot. Over time, the crack grew wider and deeper, but Victoria chose to ignore it. When she walked down that street, she crossed to the other side and looked the other way.

On this particular day, Victoria could no longer ignore the gaping hole. She stood at the edge and peered down into what was now a sinkhole, a good two feet below the surface. As she studied the hole, she lost her footing and toppled in, head first. She sat upright and struggled to make it to her knees, but she was starting to sink.

Victoria attempted to crawl to the edge, certain she could pull herself up, but with each movement, she sank deeper into the muck. She neared the edge when the soft earth gave way. Within seconds, she was up to her neck and gasping for breath.

She opened her mouth to scream for help, but it was too late; Victoria was pulled below the surface, and the earth closed in over her head. Deeper and deeper she sunk, and as quickly as it sucked her in, the earth spit her out. She landed on her backside in the dark.

Victoria stood up and put her hands out in front of her, moving forward until she met with a smooth rock wall. Feeling her way along the wall, she came to an adjacent wall and then another. She was at the end of a tunnel. Terrified, she turned around and stepped into the unknown.

Her eyes adjusted just enough to keep from running into the sides of the tunnel as it twisted and turned. Up ahead she saw light coming from a small opening in the tunnel wall.

Bending down, Victoria peeked into a spacious cave. At the far end of the lit, cave room sat an old woman at a rickety table, dabbing at her eyes with a worn handkerchief.

Victoria moved inside and stood up. The old woman didn't seem to notice her, so Victoria walked softly toward her and stood near the table. Eventually, the old woman glanced up at her with lifeless eyes.

She slowly stood and hobbled to a pot-bellied stove, and began to stir something that smelled dreadful. Victoria asked the old woman what she was doing in the cave, but she didn't respond.

The old woman set the spoon down and moved painfully to a single bed that sat opposite the room from the stove. She perched herself on the edge of the bed and gently retrieved a framed photo from the nightstand.

The old woman patted the bed beside her, and Victoria sat down carefully. They sat in silence for a few moments while the old woman gently ran her fingers over the chipped picture frame and deliberately traced the outline of the young girl in the photo.

Victoria looked around the room, which was several times larger than the tiny living area where the old woman had placed her things. Dozens of faded photographs hung on a nearby wall.

Still clutching the photo, the old woman finally spoke, "This is why I'm here; she's my daughter."

"What happened to her?" Victoria asked.

The old woman's body tensed and a lone tear dripped down her cheek.

"She's lost, I guess. I mean, I haven't seen her in years. That's what I'm doing here; waiting."

She placed the photo back onto the nightstand and clasped her hands together. Victoria was puzzled; the hands looked familiar, yet she had never seen this woman.

Tears began to stream down the old woman's face. Victoria instinctively reached for the familiar hand, but the old woman pulled it away and gestured toward the photo wall.

"They don't understand," she said.

Victoria got up and moved to the wall, scanning the photos. Groups of people smiled and laughed, arms slung around each other. The old woman was much younger in the photos.

"Why are you waiting here alone? Why not go back and wait with them?" Victoria nodded toward the wall of photos where she was standing.

"Nobody understands how much I miss her. They want me to go on without her, but I can't; she's all I care about now."

The old woman began to sob. Suddenly a black cloud appeared from behind her. It swirled around her midsection, gaining speed as it covered more of her body. With each revolution, a tip of the black cloud stabbed at her chest, causing her to cry out in agony.

Victoria stepped backward until she was plastered against the photo wall. A picture crashed down, and the glass broke at her feet, but she never took her eyes off the old woman.

"What's happening?" Victoria shouted.

"Get out of her, now!" demanded the old woman.

"Wait, let me help you," Victoria pleaded.

"Leave me alone, please," cried the old woman.

Victoria stepped toward the black cloud that now enshrouded the old woman. Although she couldn't see her anymore, she could make out the outline of the old woman's body. Sobs came from somewhere inside the blackness.

"I want to be alone, please go now!" the old woman pleaded.

Victoria glanced at the hole in the wall on the far side of the cave and back at the screaming black cloud. Not sure what to do, she finally turned away from the old woman and ran toward the tunnel opening. Victoria bent down to exit the cave, when a large mirror above the hole caught her attention.

Her heart was pounding, and she needed to get out of there... to find her way back home, but she was mesmerized by the mirror; its gold frame encrusted with precious stones.

She could hear the old woman's faint cries from the back of the cave.

Reaching out to touch the frame, Victoria was startled by her hand, the same hand she had noticed on the old woman. She stepped in front of the mirror and gasped. Staring back at her was the old woman.

The Forgotten Wall

I was becoming the Old Woman in the Cave. It wasn't just that I missed my daughter every single day, but I was desperate to have her back. I couldn't seem to focus fully for any length of time on much else. I was distracted by memories, agonized over what may never be, and terrified of what was still to come.

The more I focused on Jordan, the sadder and lonelier I became. I lived with that imaginary black cloud over my heart, and it was getting darker by the day. I was retreating into my cave, my self-imposed prison. The black cloud of depression was beginning to suffocate me. The photos on my wall were beginning to fade. If I didn't take drastic measures to re-focus, I too was going to have a wall of forgotten people.

It is natural to focus on what we have lost, and we have every right to grieve, for a time. You enter the danger zone when you're singularly focused on the loss or pain for so long that it begins to interfere with or destroy your other relationships. The very relationships you need to help you out of your cave. You may be in danger of ending up with a Forgotten Wall of loved ones.

Consider who might wind up on your Forgotten Wall.

 Are you at risk of becoming the old woman (or man) in the cave?

Focus Board

Our minds have the power to create images that can either help or hurt us. Since actions begin with thoughts, then what we think about is important. Not only does visualization affect your attitude, but also your actions. Therefore, be careful to create the proper images in your mind. It will become nearly impossible to heal if the only images you allow into your mind are those that are at the center of your pain, your loss, your Beast.

You have the ability to think about whatever you want, so begin to re-create images that will inspire and support your victory over the Beast. First thing in the morning, give yourself time to focus and reflect on what you have. Say a prayer of thanksgiving and get your mind focused on the people and situations that will help you to move forward; to heal.

In the beginning stages of your re-focusing process, it will be tremendously helpful to create some tangible images that you can

211

gravitate toward to help you to stay focused on the right things. Consider creating a Focus Board, which is a collage of images that serve as your visual reminders.

Perhaps you have created a vision or a goal board. A Focus Board is similar, but there is an important difference. The purpose of a vision or goal board is for you to visualize what you want to attract and achieve in your future. Some of the things on your Focus Board are indeed future-oriented, but a Focus Board is more about what needs and deserves your focus TODAY. To get to the future, you have to get through the day. A Focus Board can help. When I'm tempted to focus too much on Jordan or to head into fear mode, I re-focus on the people, places, and things that are on my Focus Board. Here are some examples of images on my Focus Board:

- My family and extended family.
- My husband and son who are huge San Francisco 49er fans, at a game.
- Photos of me with Rich.
- My goddaughter and namesake. Her photo reminds me to be the woman her parents want their daughter to be like.
- Jordan, in happier times.
- A photo of a rainbow that I took in my backyard.

- My cat Shiska - he has been by my side through it all.
- Inspirational photographs, e.g., a photo of a little boy running on prosthetic legs, pure joy spread across his face, with the captions reading: "Your Excuse is Invalid."
- Mountains - the majesty inspires me, and I love hiking.
- Inspirational quotes and reminders.
- Some of the places I want to visit. Although this is more future centered, it reminds me now to keep my passion for travel, and that my traveling days are not over.
- The Rockin' Redhead logo, which encourages me to stay focused on my mission of making meaning from the madness.
- A heart with the words: "I'm not afraid of the future because God is already there." It helps me to replace fear with faith.
- My great-niece. Her photo reminds me that although life is full of loss, it is also full of joy.

You get the idea. Glue images onto a poster board and have it laminated to keep everything secure.

Since I spend a great deal of time in my home office, I have mine on my office wall. If you work outside the home and have a space for it, place it on the wall there. If not, you could create a small photo album, a digital version to serve as a screen saver, or a series of images on your smart phone. Consider creating two Focus Boards; one for home and one for your place of work.

No matter what type of Focus Board you choose, be certain it is easily accessible and that you use it.

You Are More Than a _____

You are more than what you are going through, more than your Beast. When reality sunk in, and I had to admit I was the mother of a heroin addict, it hurt. We put labels on people, and on situations. I didn't want the label - **mother of an addict.**

Whether or not people realize it, they judge you. There is a stigma attached to drug addiction and mental illness that also follows the families, especially the parents. I no longer allow myself to be defined by the stigma that is placed on me due to my daughter's disease.

At a time when I was missing Jordan, when the hole in my heart for her was so big that I could barely breathe, my sister-in-law wrote me this note. She reminded me that I'm far more than the mother of an addict.

Val,

You are my sister and my friend. You are energetic, bold, clever and beautiful. You are a daughter. You are supportive. You love the family, and sacrifice to serve the family.

You are a wife. You are sexy, hard-headed, and loyal. Richie digs you. You are a mother. Fiercely protective, nurturing, and carry the history of your children's lives with you in your heart. You are the bow to their arrows, and your bow is strong and true. Sometimes arrows fly, unexpected, to places never intended. They may be lost for a time, until they are recovered. They may be scuffed and rusty, the feathers torn and tattered. But if returned to you, you would do your best to prepare them for flight again.

Lastly, you are Valerie. A little girl, with hopes and wild dreams that has grown into an impeccable woman who walks this earth with pride and pain, beauty and uncertainty, and a most contagious spirit.

I love you Val,

Suz

You are more than a label. You are more than your child's addiction or your father's disgrace. You are more than your mistakes, the past, or your battle. You are strong, courageous, and valuable. Your future is full of potential and possibility.

Fill in the blanks below as a reminder of all that you are.

I, _____ *am a*

_____,

but I am more than that. I am also _____

_____

_____

_____

_____

Fitting the Pieces Together

When you **Adjust Your Focus** away from troubles, you will be in a better mindset to **Stand On Your Story** and **Make Meaning From the Madness.** If you are knocked down, keeping your focus will allow you to once again, **Decide to Stand Up and Fight.** Proper focus will give you energy to **Get On Your Spiritual Armor** and **Put On Your Oxygen Mask.** Since you **Build Your Circle of Strength** with other people, your sole focus will no longer be on yourself or your Beast. Proper focus is necessary to **Change Your Attitude** and to keep it positive. Until you're properly focused, it will be very difficult to **Stop Being a Control Freak.**

Battle Reminders

Keep your social media microscope in proper focus.

Remember that everybody has a story.

Stop playing the same movie and expecting a different ending.

Avoid the cycle of hope and massive disappointment by revising the expectations you have of others.

Don't become the old woman (or man) in the cave.

Who is at risk of ending up on your Forgotten Wall?

Create a Focus Board.

Believe you are more than a _____.

Action #7: Stop Being a Control Freak

"If you're trying to save someone from themselves,
consider retiring your cape. I put my Supermom Cape
on so many times that it is ripped, stained, and frayed. It
has been caught in doors, stuck in my underwear, and
wrapped around my neck. It was time to take it off."

— *Valerie Silveira*

Power in Letting Go

For the longest time, I thought my influence over Jordan would be enough to make her change. After she had been shot, I was certain my love and encouragement would remind her of who she was. Once she was deep into her addiction, I still thought that there was something I could say that would make a difference. I searched for the perfect phrase, scripture, or words of wisdom. I thought I could find the right thing to say or do that would turn on the lightbulb in her brain, and it would be the moment everything began to turn around for Jordan, for me. I said and did anything and everything I could think of to try to make her change; to return to my Jordan, whom I was longing to have back. I finally had to realize Jordan's addiction is one of the things I cannot change.

The Serenity Prayer

"God, grant me the serenity to accept the things I cannot change, the courage to change the things I can, and the wisdom to know the difference."

— Unknown

The Serenity Prayer is a prayer for everyone, a mantra for which we should all strive. I have constantly prayed for the serenity to accept the things I cannot change. I have prayed for the courage to change myself in the middle of the worst period of my life. It's the third part of this prayer that might be the most challenging - the wisdom to know the difference. The difference between what we can change and what we cannot.

Incredible amounts of energy go into failed attempts at changing a situation you don't have the power to change; the same energy that could be used to change something you can. You can change your attitude, focus, relationships, and faith. You can change your fitness, how much you forgive, and how you think. You can change the way you speak to and about others, and the way you speak to yourself. The bottom line is that the only person you can change is you.

It is said the definition of insanity is: doing the same thing over and over and expecting a different result. **My definition of insanity is, trying to change something or someone you can't change.**

The real power is in letting go of what you cannot change and working on what you can. Pray for, and work toward gaining the wisdom to know the difference between the things you cannot change and the things you can.

 Have you expended effort trying to change someone or something you cannot change?

The "F" Word Will Set You Free

Start using the "F" word. If you have been living with or battling a Beast, you need to use the "F" word. Not that "F" word, although you may have used that one too. The "F" word I am referring to is Forgiveness.

"Forgiveness is unlocking the door

to set someone free

and realizing you were the prisoner."

—Max Lucado

Forgiving may be one of the biggest obstacles you come up against, and once you learn to do it often, it will be one of the most powerful things you ever do. Forgiving another person for an offense can seem as if we are excusing the behavior, so we choose not to forgive. Instead, we become angry, resentful, and bitter. Holding onto anger and resentment rarely results in hurting or changing another person. We only hurt ourselves.

Start Using the "F" Word All the Time

When The Guy shot my daughter, I wanted him to suffer. *I . . . wanted . . . him . . . to . . . suffer!* I was the mama bear, and my cub had nearly been killed. I was hurt and scared. I wanted him to pay for what he did, and I carried that anger around for a long time, even after he was convicted and sent to prison.

According to the law, The Guy *was* paying for what he did, but that wasn't good enough for me. Jordan had changed, and I

223

blamed him. For the three years leading up to the shooting, Jordan had made terrible decisions, some having nothing to do with The Guy. It didn't matter, I wanted and needed to blame someone other than Jordan, and The Guy was the obvious choice.

The Guy had no idea how angry I was with him or whether or not I had forgiven him. If he had known, he probably wouldn't have cared. Who was I punishing? Me.

The Guy was not the only one in prison. I was locked up in my self-imposed prison of unforgiveness. Once I came to that realization, I opened the prison door, and slowly set myself free.

Expending energy holding onto anger is foolish. When you're battling a Beast, you will need all of your energy focused in the right direction. Don't waste any of it living with anger and resentment as a result of your unwillingness to forgive.

Are you holding back on forgiveness? If you are, open the prison doors and set yourself free.

Give Yourself a Pardon

The "F" word may be harder to say to yourself than it is to say to others, even people who have hurt you deeply. Sometimes the difficulty lies in the uncertainty of why you need to forgive yourself. It may be that you are attempting to blame yourself unnecessarily.

For the better part of thirteen years, I picked myself apart, in an attempt to pinpoint the cause of Jordan's behavior, and eventually, her addiction. Separating me from my child proved nearly impossible. I was a single parent for many of Jordan's formidable years, and therefore concluded there must have been something I did or didn't do that caused Jordan's disease. It had to be my fault she jumped onto her Roller Coaster From Hell.

At the very least, I had to be a contributor. It didn't matter that Jordan didn't blame me, or that my family and friends told me I was a great mother. Nothing anyone said could keep me from the mental and emotional abuse I piled on myself.

It proved much easier for me to even forgive Jordan for her choices than it was for me to forgive myself for something I had yet to figure out. Mama and papa bears find it much simpler to point the finger at themselves than at their cubs. When teenagers and adult children cause a mother terrible pain and heartbreak, she will give herself whiplash turning the other cheek. Wives will forgive abusive husbands until they are blue (or black) in the face. Granting self-forgiveness can be very difficult.

You may have made some very bad choices in the past. Maybe you have caused the people you love a great deal of pain. If you have already asked the people you have hurt for forgiveness, but are continuing to withhold forgiveness from yourself, then you're *choosing* the prison of unforgiveness.

We have all made mistakes. There are plenty of choices I have made, things I have said, or actions I have taken for which I am not proud. Most people will tell you if they had it to do over, they would do things the same way. I wonder if that is true. I would go back and do many things very differently.

Whether you would choose to change the past or not, you can't. You can't change a single second of the past, but you can choose to forgive yourself. Until you can find a way to forgive yourself, it will be difficult for you to forgive anybody else.

In our attempts to control a very out-of-control situation, we attempt to control others. Maybe not the direct actions or behaviors of others, but sometimes we try to control what others think or feel.

I was caught in between what I assumed people thought or felt about Jordan and how I felt about her. Since I was enabling her and trying to control her behavior, I remained convinced she was going to turn the corner at any moment and my family would be whole again. Therefore, I wanted to be sure, when she did, she would be welcomed back with open arms by everyone.

It's not easy to separate ourselves from our families and especially our children. We believe they are a reflection of their upbringing and therefore of us. If the apple doesn't fall far from the tree, how could Jordan be in another orchard?

When someone goes off the rails, we are all guilty of jumping to conclusions about their family. Everyone is curious about the parents of a school shooter or a serial killer. After an unimaginable event, it's natural to look for answers in an attempt to reconcile what has happened, and the entire family ends up under a microscope.

It isn't much different with addicts. People want to find an easy answer as to why the addiction manifested, whose DNA it came from, or what happened to cause the addiction. We go looking for answers, and the first stop is the family. In certain cases, family actions could have a great deal to do with how a child turns out or whether or not they wind up addicted to drugs or alcohol.

Many addicts or people who make very bad choices come from good homes. Unfortunately, people continue to jump to conclusions without understanding the complicated disease of addiction or other factors. I had jumped to those same conclusions many times before I had an addicted child.

It hurts when a family member acts in ways that are opposed to your values or expectations. You have a connection to your loved ones, so when they do something dishonest, or worse, there is a part of you that feels a certain sense of responsibility. Every fiber of your being becomes defensive, even if you're sickened by their actions. It feels like a direct hit, when a negative comment or feeling has been launched at your child.

The actions of your family members, even your children, are not your actions. People may judge you because of the actions of your child, husband, brother, mother, aunt, or another family member. There is nothing you can do about it, so let them play judge and jury. Just as we can't control the behavior of our loved ones, we can't control the thoughts or feelings that other people have about those loved ones.

It may be that you are assuming people are more judgmental than they are, or that they are thinking about you far more than they are. When my children were overly concerned about what others were thinking, I would tell them:

"Don't spend so much time thinking about what others are thinking about you. They don't spend nearly as much time thinking about you, as you do thinking about them thinking about you."

The amount of self-contempt, judgment, and guilt you pile on yourself may far be more than what anyone else will send your way. In any case, let it go.

"F" Them

The day I got the call informing me The Guy was released from the county jail and into the hands of the state correctional system, I didn't react the way I had thought I would. I didn't throw my arms up and cheer. I never had the party I claimed I was going to throw. Instead, I bawled like a baby.

I held my face in my hands and pictured The Guy. I saw him in a prison jumpsuit, with hands and ankles shackled; acting tough as fear took over every fiber of his being. It overwhelmed me to think about the once innocent baby whose life path brought him to a state of mind where he would abuse girls and fire a gun into a house full of people. Nineteen years after the innocent baby entered the world, he was headed to a state penitentiary.

Instead of feeling vindicated, I wept for the situation, and I forgave The Guy.

Then I took it back.

Use the "F" Word All the Time

"When asked how many times a brother should be
forgiven for sinning against Him, Jesus replied, I don't
say to you seven times but seventy-seven times."
(Matthew 18:21-22)

Even after you forgive someone, something might trigger an old feeling, and like I did with The Guy, you will snatch your forgiveness back as quickly as you gave it.

Forgiveness lightens the load you're carrying, so resist the urge to grab it back after you have given it away. If you keep taking back the forgiveness you have let go of, and piling it back onto yourself, before long, you have a new thousand pound Beast on your shoulders.

There is no expiration date on forgiveness, so just keep at it. The important thing is to keep forgiving until you have nothing left to forgive.

Forgiving the Source of Your Pain

It took me some time to forgive Jordan. I now understand she has a disease, but my frustration over her reluctance to treat her disease left me, among so many other emotions, angry. When someone has a disease affecting another part of the body, they seek treatment. People take insulin, heart medication and use a whole host of other options to treat diseases. With drug addiction, the disease seems to repel treatment, making it harder for the patient to seek help.

Drug addiction is a Beast, a very large one. I hate drug addiction. I hate Jordan's Beast, but I love Jordan so I had a hard time separating the two. My reluctance to forgive her was the age-old concern that forgiveness somehow excuses or justifies the behavior. I had no intention of forgiving the drug addiction Beast; why should I?

The answer is simple; Jordan's Beast is part of her, and therefore I had to forgive the whole thing. I forgave her for the lies, deceit, and for her unwillingness to fight. I forgave her for bringing danger and violence into our lives. I forgave her for wasting our money, ruining holidays and birthdays, and breaking my heart over and over again. I forgave her for tearing apart the thing I so desperately wanted back together - my family. I forgave her for all of it.

If I didn't forgive Jordan's drug addiction Beast, I couldn't have completely forgiven her. Had I not been able to forgive her, it would have been much more difficult to forgive myself.

Forgiving something as big and evil as Jordan's Beast, made it easier for me to forgive myself and to forgive others. Let go of anger and resentment. Whether or not another party is guilty, be generous with forgiveness, and it will pave the way for much healing. Believe it or not, forgiving your Beast may be a stepping stone to removing him from your life.

Recognize the absolute necessity to forgive. Forgiveness is for *you*; let God deal with others. Let them deal with themselves. Let the justice system deal with them. Let their journey take them where it needs to take them. Use the "F" Word!

Are you having a hard time forgiving yourself or others?

It's Not All About You

Parents feel a certain degree of responsibility for their child's actions, even after those children are adults. Not only did I gladly strap on my Supermom Cape repeatedly, but I felt it was *my duty*. You may have similar thoughts and feelings about a spouse, parent, or another loved one.

A few of my friends feel as if their ex-husband's new wives have benefitted at their expense. They will say, "It's not fair she gets him after I'm the one who went through all of the crap that made him a better husband!" It probably isn't fair if one chooses to look at it in that way.

Our part in another person's journey can be significant in allowing that person to mature, or grow. There should be some peace in knowing you had a hand in helping another person in their learning process. It is little solace when the wounds are fresh, but over time, it is important to find your way there.

As painful as your experience may have been, it does provide you an opportunity to learn and grow. I sacrificed a great deal attempting to help Jordan, so naturally I wanted to be the person standing next to her when she finds her way. It isn't just that I

233

sacrificed and tried to help; after all, I wasn't the only person who helped Jordan, but she is *my* daughter.

If Jordan finds a way to beat her Beast and one day stands in victory over it, I may not be the one standing with her, but does it really matter?

Whether or not you are the sacrificial lamb in somebody else's journey, in the end it's their journey. It may hurt to hear this, but another person's journey is not about you, just as Jordan's is not about me.

Excruciatingly Painful Love

If you run into a bear, you are in trouble. If you run into a mama bear with her cubs, you are dead.

When Sean was in fifth grade, the school had a lockdown. It had been reported that a man with a shotgun was seen near the playground of the school. Once the lockdown was over, I picked up Sean and a couple of his friends and drove them to our home.

We lived a mile or so from the school in a neighborhood just off the main road that divided several housing developments. Between the main road and our back yard was a greenbelt. After an event such as a school lockdown, adrenalin is running high, to say the least. It didn't take long for my overactive mind to convince myself the gunman had evaded capture by hiding in the greenbelt.

Driving up our street, I conjured up visions of the mad gun-toting man hiding in our house. My heart raced as I grabbed a golf club from the garage and charged into the house. I went room to room, golf club in the air, daring this imaginary intruder to mess with me.

By the time I made it downstairs, Sean and his friends were behind me laughing. I seriously don't know what I would have done had an intruder jumped out at me from behind a shower curtain pointing a shotgun at me. What I do know is that I felt powerful and fearless because I was protecting my cub, and his friends.

The majority of moms are not much different from a mama bear. Mess with me and you might have trouble, but don't mess with my kids. We are incredibly protective of our children. There was no doubt in my mind I would have protected my son, at the potential cost of my life.

Dealing with hardships, heartbreak, loss, and pain is a battle. When the person responsible for causing your pain is your child, you can become paralyzed. We are wired to provide for and protect our children. When they are in trouble, we are the mama bear (or daddy bear) fiercely fighting for our cubs.

What do you do when you raise your weapon to defend your child, and it is the child staring back at you?

When we make tough parenting decisions, it is called tough love. Walking away from a child who is on a freight train headed for a brick wall isn't tough, it is excruciating.

Tough love is not allowing your child to go to the movies on Friday night. Taking a stand with a child is not easy, which is why it is called "tough love." Pulling out the safety net and allowing my only daughter to crash has not been tough, it has been excruciating. I call it *excruciatingly painful love.*

Letting Jordan fall is without question, one of the hardest things I have ever done, but also the right thing. A few years back Jordan screamed, *"It's my* life!" She was right, it is her life. Unfortunately, though, her life choices have an impact on many other people. Each person is responsible for their choices, for who they become. Although your journey is uniquely yours, it's important to remember how interwoven your life is with others' lives.

I feared if I turned away from Jordan, she might forget how much I love her. She may think she has nobody left and, therefore, give up. I shared that sentiment with my friend, Teresa, whose daughter has been in a battle with a drug addiction Beast. Teresa sent me this text:

> *"Sweetheart, you have proven and proven and proven... did I say proven...your love for your girl; unconditional, not based on her behavior or merit. She knows this, and she may call you a bitch when you resist her attempts to control you, but deep down in her 'knower,' she has been loved by you as only a mother can love, and that is all truth that even in the height of selfishness she can't deny."*

People, especially addicts, who have been using us for a long time, can make us feel obligated to continue in the Cycle of Hope and Disappointment. As my friend Teresa said, deep down in their "knower," they know you love them and have been there for them more than they had a right to expect. There is no need for you to prove it over and over again.

If It Were Possible, It Would Be Done

Are you exhausting yourself in an effort to save someone from themselves? I was desperate to save my daughter from herself - to battle her drug Beast for her. Jordan told me what I wanted to hear. Things were always going to change *in a couple of weeks*. Drug addicts lie to keep you in the game - the enabling game. She strung me along, took advantage of my generosity and my love. She was smart and knew exactly how to get me to keep believing the lies, or at least wanting to believe them. Ultimately, it was my choice to keep believing her Beast.

The reality that hit me one day was this: **If it were possible for me to save Jordan from herself, I would have done it long ago!**

If all it took was effort, money, tears, sleepless nights, and love...it would have been over years ago. It was then that I took a step back and surveyed the situation. No matter that my heart had been shattered into a million pieces. I could allow it to be shattered into a million and one pieces, and the situation would remain the same. The harsh reality is that I can't save my daughter; she has to save herself.

You cannot save someone either. Your loved ones have choices, but so do you.

Taking Off the Cape

Love is the reason you strap on your Supermom or Super_____(fill in the blank) Cape in the first place, but fear is what keeps it tied around your neck. You want to be ready at all times, just in case your loved one needs you. If your loved one is involved in self-destructive behavior, the chances are you will use it so often you may as well leave it on.

It was time; I knew I needed to take off my Supermom Cape. Deep down, I knew my enabling disguised as helping, was not helping Jordan. By the time I realized it, the Cape had been on for years, and there was a big knot in it, which would require some effort to remove it. I took out the scissors, but I couldn't get my hands to work. My head knew it was the right thing to do, but my heart was in control of the scissors.

I finally got my heart in agreement with my head and made the cut. I did it for me, and for Jordan. She needs to find her own way, and I was tired of riding the Roller Coaster from Hell. The Cape was so worn out there was nothing much left of it. I ran my fingers over the rips and tears, and poked my fingers through the holes. I gently stroked the tattered edges and folded it up neatly.

Then panic set in, what if I needed it again? I didn't trust myself, so I gave the Cape to Rich, for safekeeping. He probably burned it. I came clean with my husband and stopped hiding my enabling and codependent behavior from him.

Depending upon how long you have worn your Cape, it may feel strange once you take it off. When I took mine off, it felt as if a part of me was missing. I had worn that Cape for more than a decade. A part of me *was* missing, but an even bigger part of me was free. I was no longer a party to Jordan's drug addiction.

A mom of an addict wrote to me about her daughter:

> *"She has told me repeatedly that she doesn't have an addiction. I have thought maybe I should try to get help, do more for her. Then I think, who am I kidding? I have tried that. So it's time to enjoy all the wonderful blessings in my life, turn her over to God and on with life. I also realized that she is not ready for help yet. I'm ready for help and healing; that's what I have to focus on."*

If you are wearing a Cape in an effort to save another person, take out the scissors and cut the string that binds you to your Cape. If you don't, not only will you practically hang yourself with it, but you will also continue to prevent your loved one from learning what they need to learn. Understand you had good intentions, and forgive yourself if you wore it far too long.

Fitting the Pieces Together

It is not easy to **Stop Being a Control Freak. You** will most certainly need the other Actions to support your efforts, just as you will need to let go of control in order to successfully implement the other Actions. You will need to loosen your grip enough to allow yourself to **Decide to Stand Up and Fight** and to **Get On Your Spiritual Armor.** When you attempt to control things you can't control you will exhaust yourself before you have a chance to **Put On Your Oxygen Mask.** In order to **Build Your**

Circle of Strength, you will need to place your trust in others, which is impossible to do when you are trying to control everything. Being a control freak will affect your ability to **Change Your Attitude** and to **Adjust Your Focus.** How will you **Stand On Your Story** and **Make Meaning From the Madness** if you don't allow yourself to be vulnerable, to learn, and to grow?

Battle Reminders

Pray and live the Serenity Prayer.

Forgive yourself.

Forgive others.

Forgive the source of your pain.

When you take your forgiveness back, forgive again.

Another person's journey is not about you.

Take off your Cape.

Action #8: Stand On Your Story

*"It's easy to be your best when everything is going right.
It's when life smacks you upside the head with a two-by-
four that you discover what you are made of."*

— Valerie Silveira

"Some Things Don't Make Sense" File

You set goals, plan, strive, and push to make your life all that you imagined it could be, and then life whacks you upside the head with the proverbial two-by-four. It was nowhere in my plans or dreams that one day my incredibly gifted daughter would be lost in the belly of her drug addiction Beast. My goals didn't include living with my Beast.

Jordan never planned for her life to be where she is today. Nobody says, "When I grow up, I'm going to be a drug addict." Not one parent thinks, "I can't wait for this little precious baby to shatter my heart." You will never hear a woman say, "I cannot wait to be married and abused by my husband."

"Life is what happens to you while you're busy making
other plans."
— *"Beautiful Boy" by John Lennon*

We all start out in life with hopes and dreams, and then life happens. If life has happened to you while you were busy making other plans, then you will need to make new plans and dream new dreams.

Have you ever thought "this really can't be happening," or "this can't be my life?" You are not alone. I know approximately one person whose life appears to be going exactly as planned. I hope that she has flexibility built into her life plan, as not even she will escape life without hardship, trials, or heartbreak.

At times, I still have those out of body experiences where I can't believe what has happened. The other day I was discussing something with a family member, when I felt the waves of disbelief come crashing in one more time. I heard myself speaking, yet found it hard to believe the words were coming out of my mouth, even though I have been dealing with it for years.

We are all looking for a place to file things in our minds. We agonize over tragedies or a sudden loss, finding it hard to reconcile what has happened, to what we anticipated or expected.

When something happens that you aren't sure where to file in your mind, you need to make a new file. Let's call the new file, "Some Things Don't Make Sense." That is where I have begun to file the drug addiction Beast nightmare.

Filing your tragedy or pain somewhere in your mind will not necessarily lessen the ache in your heart, but it may provide some peace, allowing you to begin to accept what has happened.

Stand <u>On</u> Your Story

When you experience a sudden tragedy or an ongoing agony, you will change. I am not the same person I was before all hell broke loose. Two decades ago, when Jordan was still innocent, and I had nothing but hope for the future, for her future, I was different than I am today. You are different than you were before all hell broke loose in your life.

Your life's two-by-four has changed you; living with a Beast has challenged you in ways you could not have imagined. Life experiences change us. It is up to us to decide what they will change us into.

Your Battle will also change you, and it can change you in positive ways that may be hard to see right now. I would be lying if I said I was glad things have happened the way they have. I'm not thankful Jordan slipped away, was shot, or became a drug addict. If it were possible, I would rewind the clock and change my story in a heartbeat. You probably wish you could turn your clock back too.

Since turning back the clock is not possible, we must own what has happened without shame or guilt. You need not stand in the muck of your story, like a victim after a storm. Stand up tall,

248

put your shoulders back, and declare that you are going to become a better person, not in spite of your story, but because of your story.

Resist the temptation to wallow in self-pity, shame, guilt, or fear. Fight the urge to give up, or to give in. Reject the notion that you have *become* your story. Refuse to stay down on the mat. Shake off the stigma that society has thrown at you. Dig down and find the courage to become the person you would not have become had you not been a part of your own life's story.

A mantra used by Alcoholics Anonymous and Narcotics Anonymous is: "One Day at a Time." This is good advice not only for someone in recovery, but it is great advice for everyone to live by. It's especially important to live by this philosophy when dealing with a Beast. Your battle may seem overwhelming, so projecting too far into the future can paralyze your progress.

Jesus said, "Do not worry about tomorrow, for tomorrow will worry about itself. Each day has enough trouble of its own." We should have a healthy concern for the future since we will live the rest of our lives there. It becomes problematic when we are so focused on the future that we forget to live for today.

When going through a rough period you will spend a great deal of time trying to figure everything out. Remember that a situation that may seem impossible now may work itself out as the future unfolds.

God's advice is to concern ourselves with today, not tomorrow. You don't need to figure everything out today. The only thing you have to figure out <u>today</u> is what you can do <u>today</u>.

 Are you focused on today?

In a conversation with a treatment center, I explained some of Jordan's symptoms, but before I could finish, she said,

"That's heroin."

It was like being punched in the gut. A child's addiction is never easy for a parent to hear or to accept. Nobody wants their child to go through the struggle of addiction; no parent wants their child to live with a Beast. When Jordan admitted her drug addiction, it was to Oxycodone. It hurt, but at least her Beast now had a name - drug addiction.

All drug addiction is serious, but what the treatment center staffer said, took my breath away. To my knowledge, I had never known anyone who used heroin. It brought to mind images of strung out people in movies, lying in abandoned buildings with rubber tubing tied around their arms. That wasn't Jordan.

It would take some time for me to say the "H" word out loud and a bit longer to say it in a sentence with Jordan's name. Eventually, I shed the guilt and shame and can admit it because it's true and because it's only one of the many things that make up the person who is Jordan.

There are things you have learned or had to face that have taken your breath away too. I wish I didn't have to use the words heroin and Jordan in the same sentence, but it is part of her story and, as a result, it is part of mine. As painful as it has been, I own that part of my story. You will need to do the same. Hiding from sad realities or being ashamed of them, only makes your battle more difficult.

Stop Skipping School

Did you ever skip school? I did. I had no interest in science and yawned during geography. Just because I made an A, or a B didn't mean I had retained what I learned. My philosophy was, information in long enough to make the grade, and then information out. Of course, I retained a great deal, but not enough. I should have taken school more seriously; I probably shouldn't have skipped so many classes.

As we go through life, we are always in school. You will find teachers everywhere: at work, on television or your computer, in social circles, at the grocery store, and even at home. Words of wisdom can be found in books, videos, movies, on the internet, and coming out of the mouth of a child. Too often, we skip the class and miss the lesson.

Some of the most valuable lessons you will ever learn will be through your trials. One of your life's best teachers may be your Beast.

While I was merely putting up with my Beast, I couldn't have cared less about learning much from my experience; I simply wanted it to stop. I desperately needed my daughter back, I wanted my family to be whole again, and I wanted relief from the agony.

As I began to battle, I understood there were lessons to learn, so I got ready. I put on my best dress, grabbed my books, and headed to "school." My pencils were sharpened, my notebook empty, the pages of my lesson books crisp. I was eager to learn.

Before long, the class became demanding and painful. It didn't take long before my eagerness to learn the lesson waned. It was all I could do to open the book, so I started to skip the class. Soon, I was skipping school altogether.

The most challenging lessons in life's school are those that involve emotions. I don't mind the challenge of solving a problem, but once the heart is involved, an ordinary lesson turns into a trigonometry class.

Some of our lessons in life have been incredibly painful. The lessons you learn while riding your Roller Coaster From Hell and from battling your Beast will be the most painful, yet the most valuable. Much of what I learned, I did so, kicking and screaming. You can skip class all you want and even flunk the grade, but you will be put right back where you started until you learn the lesson.

It may seem impossible in your current situation, for anything good to come of it. This may be especially true if there is no closure in sight. I know firsthand what it is to put your life on hold while your world is falling apart. My daughter is still an addict. Now and then, she gets "clean" for short periods of time. While I feel a sense of hope, I temper that hope with the reality that there is a likelihood of a relapse to follow.

You may be angry and feel as if life has dealt you a pretty unfair hand. I encourage you to take a deep breath and be open to the possibility of learning some valuable lessons. This type of personal growth cannot be learned by reading a book or hearing a story. Unfortunately, you will never learn from others' battles, what you can from your own.

 Have you been skipping "school?"

From Beast to Best

It's easy to be your best when everything is going right. It is when life smacks you upside the head with that two-by-four that you discover what you're made of. We rarely grow when things are going our way. Why would we? You have never been in a better position to become the best version of yourself than you are right now.

For a few years, we lived on Key Biscayne, a small island in the Biscayne Bay off the shore from Miami. We were never in a hurricane; however, we did experience quite a few strong tropical storms. After near hurricane force winds, surprisingly most of the palm trees were still standing. Palm trees are tremendously flexible. In fact, they can bend right down to the ground without breaking. What is even more interesting is that after the storm batters and bends the palm tree, it comes out of the storm stronger than it was before.

You are similar to the palm tree. The Beast can bring a storm into your life and even bend you to your breaking point, but with an attitude of flexibility and determination, you will come out stronger than you were before.

The Beast may have had you down on the mat, but ultimately the only one that can keep you down, is you. Stand up and become better and stronger than you were before all hell broke loose. No matter where you are, no matter what your Beast looks like, you can move from Beast to best.

Still Standing

You will stumble, and you will fall. It doesn't matter how many times you fall. The only thing that matters is that you get up one more time than you fall.

Your unique story has the potential to inspire and empower others. It's time for you to make the decision that no matter how many storms come upon you, like the palm tree, you will not break.

When the Beast tries to wrestle you back to the mat, laugh in his face. Be resolved that your Battle will end in victory. Be determined that when the dust settles, you will be standing over your Beast, stronger and better than you were before the battle.

Start Growing Now

Don't wait for your circumstances to change before you begin to change. The small spark that ignites your fire of change will catch like wildfire. This spark is a very small first step that will set things in motion. Change yourself, and your circumstances will change.

Although you begin to change, certain aspects of your story may not change, at least not right away. Just because I began to be a better me, didn't cause Jordan to stand up and fight. In fact, coincidentally, when I stood up to fight, Jordan was far from battling her Beast. My fight didn't have a bearing on Jordan's but had I not stood up when I did, I would have been devastated by where her life is today.

I cringe at the thought of where I would be today had I not made the decision when I did. If I had waited for Jordan's life to change for the better in order for mine to change, I would be in a world of hurt.

I repeat - don't wait for your circumstances to change before you begin to change. Start now, right where you are.

 Will you start now?

Keep the End in Mind

I know a whole lot less about life than I thought I would at my age, but I know one thing for certain - nobody is getting out alive. It's creepy to think about death. I am sure you have been awake in the dark of night thinking about death; one day you are here and in an instant, you will be gone.

Consider the legacy you will leave behind after you are gone. Think about the impact your life will have on those who love you, the people who interacted with you on your journey through life. Even if you live to a ripe old age, realistically, there will be only two or three generations who would know you well enough to remember you when you are gone. By the third generation, most of us will be a distant memory; an old family photograph.

The point here is not to cause you to become depressed, but to make you think about the legacy you are creating. You may only have two or three generations of people who remember you once you are gone, but your impact on their lives can go on for many more generations.

My goddaughter was given my middle name. Her parents told me they wanted their daughter to grow up to be like me. Initially, I was humbled and honored by those words. Then it hit me. What if she grew up to become a woman smiling on the outside, and dying on the inside? I didn't want to think about that possibility.

When your time on earth is done, what will people remember? Let us take a few minutes to consider that question. Picture your memorial service. If you prefer, read through this and then close your eyes, sit in silence and go through the process. Before you begin, let me caution you to not be too hard on yourself. Nobody is watching you go through this exercise so try not to be so humble that you forget all of the positive things that will be said about you.

Take a deep breath and picture it. Where is the service taking place - a place of worship, a country club, a private home? Possibly near a lake, along a riverbank, or on top of a mountain. As the people in your life gather to remember you, are they silent, or are they sharing memories? Through their tears, do you hear laughter; can you see their smiles as they recall their time with you?

The service is about to begin. People are making their way to their seats. Music plays in the background; what kind of music is playing; is it a particular song? The music begins to fade. In the absence of music, you hear sniffling, soft crying, an occasional sob. As you look out over the crowd, who do you see? Look at the faces of the people who have come to pay tribute to your life.

Somebody stands up to deliver your eulogy. Is it a pastor, priest, or rabbi? Is it a friend or family member; someone who knows you well? What do they say?

Once the eulogy is delivered, it's time for people representing different groups to stand up and speak. They are instructed to be completely honest and hold nothing back.

First, a family member stands and begins to speak on behalf of the family. Who is speaking and what are they saying about what you meant to the family?

Next, a friend stands up on behalf of all of your friends and explains what kind of a friend you were, and how much you will be missed. How did this person describe you?

A coworker or business associate stands next to share a side of your life most of your family and friends didn't see. Does this representative from your work life describe you as hard-working, respectful, and honest? Did the business or organization lose a valued member of the team? What do they say?

One person gets up to explain your role in a club, church, or group. What was it about you they felt compelled to share with your friends and family?

Lastly, your spouse or partner stands up. This person is trembling; finding it hard to speak. When they finally do, is it because they are overwhelmed by their loss, or because they are required to tell the truth? How do they describe your private relationship and how your loss has affected them?

As the service wraps up, from the back of the room, another person stands up and asks if they may speak for a moment. The crowd quiets and all eyes are upon this person who looks around nervously at the unfamiliar faces.

"Hello, I represent all of the store clerks, gas station attendants, restaurant servers, grocery store workers, and gardeners; all of the service providers the departed interacted with on this earth. As I'm required to speak truthfully, I must tell you that..."

How does this person describe you? Do they say you were courteous, respectful, and thankful to the people who served you in your community and beyond? Or, do they explain sadly, that you treated them rudely; that you appeared to take your unhappiness out on strangers?

It is one thing to be kind to the people we love. It is quite another for complete strangers or service people to say they will miss their interaction with you.

There were a lot of questions thrown at you and much to consider. This exercise may have been exhausting. If you feel good about how you would be remembered, then I applaud you. In your make believe memorial service, many people shared some wonderful things about you. However, it is possible a couple of things that were said made you squirm in your seat. There are aspects of our personalities we would all prefer nobody brought up. It is okay; nobody is perfect.

Here is the good news - you can change the outcome! You can't change the past, and there will always be situations you wish you could take back. If you take action now to become better, to allow yourself to grow and change, your memorial service can turn out far better than you just imagined.

 How did you feel as you went through the exercise?

Did you smile as you pictured friends and family remembering you?

Would you prefer to be remembered differently? If so, you still have time to make changes.

Fitting the Pieces Together

When you **Stand __On__ Your Story,** you will have more courage to **Decide to Stand Up and Fight** when you are knocked down. Owning your story will make it much easier to **Change Your Attitude** and to **Adjust Your Focus.** When you start to become a better version of yourself, you will automatically want to **Make Meaning From the Madness.** Standing strong will give you the perspective needed to **Put On Your Oxygen Mask, Get On Your Spiritual Armor,** and **Build Your Circle of Strength.** As you stand <u>on</u> your story, you will give yourself the strength to **Stop Being a Control Freak.**

Battle Reminders

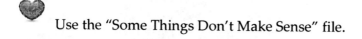
Use the "Some Things Don't Make Sense" file.

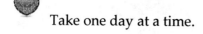
Take one day at a time.

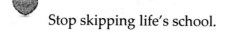
Stop skipping life's school.

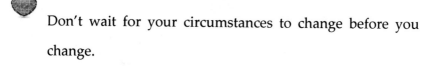
Don't wait for your circumstances to change before you change.

Keep standing.

Keep the end in mind.

Action #9: Make Meaning From the Madness

"Consider the possibility that this is the moment for which you were created."

— Valerie Silveira

It is no accident you are reading this book at this time. Before I attempt to convince you that you have what it takes to make a difference, let us take a moment to acknowledge that you feel like crap. Your heart is broken, and your soul is bruised. You are mentally, emotionally, physically, and spiritually exhausted, and I have the audacity to suggest you extend a hand to others.

You might be tempted to blow through this Action or skip it altogether. You may be convinced you're in no position to make meaning from the madness that has become your life. Did I somehow miss the reality that you have been through hell?

No, that reality has not escaped me. I have been there, and to a smaller degree, I'm still there. If I understand where you are, then how is it I could possibly believe *you* have the ability to make a difference in another person's life when you're barely holding it together yourself?

In a *million years*, I couldn't have imagined my child would become an addict, or that I would stand up and share my painful story. Perhaps you couldn't have imagined what has happened to you, but maybe there is something that can come out of your pain, something good, that you couldn't have imagined in a *million years*.

You are in a position to reach other people right where you are; the time is right for you to start making a difference because you are still battling. Yes, you heard it right. Not in spite of your circumstances, but because of where you stand right now.

People want and need to hear from real people who have been through something painful. You have credibility because of your battle. You are relatable because you are still in the battle. If you're bloodied and battle worn, yet you're still in the fight, it will give other people courage to stand up and begin to fight their own battle.

When you take one tiny step forward to reach out to someone else in need, you will get back far more than you give. It is true that we get more by giving than we do by receiving. Amazing things will begin to happen when you find the courage to share your story or to reach out to someone else.

First, you will be energized and empowered by helping others. When you share your story, your battle, at first you may not be sure what to say. Eventually, you will find wisdom pouring out of you that you were not conscious of until the words flowed from your lips. There is a fountain of knowledge, experience, and wisdom trapped inside of you just waiting to be unleashed.

There are times in which the teacher becomes the student. I have been offering guidance or wisdom to someone only to have them say something so profound that I couldn't wait to write it down. They weren't typically aware that what they said was going to be so meaningful to me. It can often be something very simple, yet brilliant. No doubt, they left the conversation wondering where in the world their own wisdom came from.

It makes no difference how old you are, or what obstacles you have faced. It is never too late, or too soon to begin to Make Meaning From the Madness.

People Are Watching You

We were selling our house in 2006. One of my brothers was helping me to paint the deck railing. It was a warm summer day, and we were each lost in our thoughts until he broke the silence.

"We were talking about you and Rich the other day."

"Yeah, what about?" I tried to act nonchalant.

While Jordan was crashing, our finances had taken a hit as well. It had been a rough few years to that point. He went on to explain that he and another brother had been discussing the strain all of this must be having on our marriage.

"We've been watching you, and we're amazed at how well you're handling everything. We can't believe you're still married. You even seem to still like each other!"

I chuckled, and then we returned to our painting. It had never occurred to me that other people were watching. I was just trying to survive. Not only were other people watching, but they were inspired. People were watching me; they were watching Rich, and they were watching us.

People are watching you, whether you realize it or not. Stand in the confident knowledge that you can come out of this stronger, wiser, and with more courage. Your resolve to stand and Battle Your Beast is not just about winning the battle; it's also about the opportunity that you have to inspire others.

Most people are intrigued by athletes, actors, or royalty. They are impressed by the people who have changed the world of sports, technology, or medicine. The masses can't seem to get enough of folks who have special talents or abilities. People are in awe of celebrities who are simply famous for being famous.

The people who inspire us most, those that captivate our hearts, are the people who have been to hell and back. The world cheers for the heroes, who have, against all odds, risen off the mat. It is the person who has battled their Beast whom we admire most. People are watching you, and they are waiting to be inspired and empowered by you.

You Don't Have to Be Mother Teresa

You may be overwhelmed at the thought of making a difference. When you think of difference makers, what types of people come to mind? Perhaps you think of social workers, visionaries, tech gurus, motivational speakers, pastors, or missionaries. Bill Gates changed the way the world communicates. Martin Luther King gave his life, spreading a message of love and equality. There are countless individuals who have made a massive difference in the lives of thousands or millions of people.

Mother Teresa made a vow of chastity, poverty, obedience, and to serve to the poorest of the poor. If you compare yourself to one of these people, you may want to pull the covers over your head and go back to sleep.

You don't have to be Mother Teresa to make a difference. Search your heart. Think of all you have been through and how much knowledge, wisdom, and personal growth you have gained. Consider your gifts and talents. Don't wait until you come up with an earth shattering venture to begin Making Meaning. Little things *are* big things.

The last thing Jordan remembers from the night she was shot was being strapped to a backboard and wheeled into an aid car. She was vomiting and going into shock.

She asked the emergency medical responder, "Am I going to die?"

He told her, "Not in my truck."

This man could have easily judged Jordan for being involved in this type of incident. He could have looked down on her for even being in that area of the city. He could have easily ignored Jordan's question, after all, he was busy trying to save her life. Instead of ignoring her question, he provided a moment of peace to a terrified girl, in what could have been her last memory.

Somehow, I hope this man finds his way to my book. I pray that realizes he is the one who drove into a neighborhood where bullets had been flying only minutes before. He will remember placing Jordan on a backboard and transporting her to Harborview Medical Center. I want him to know that at least one mother has never forgotten what he did for her daughter. I want him to know that the *little thing* he said that night was a big thing.

What little thing can you do now, that could end up being a big thing?

Begin Now

Rather than wait until you have everything figured out, which will be "never," step out and begin to Make Meaning From the Madness.

When you begin to make meaning in your life, you may find you receive much more in return than you have given. You may not see it at first, but it will happen the more time you spend in the service of others.

Go ahead and give it a try. There is one caveat though. Whatever you do, you must do it with <u>no expectation of receiving anything in return.</u> It is absolutely necessary to give with no expectation. Don't be surprised when you are repaid for your generosity and courage. Not only are others watching, but God is watching.

Don't get caught up in scorekeeping. If you never make the connection between something you did and what comes your way later, it is okay. You never know when a kind gesture now will be repaid to you down the road.

The worst case scenario is that your selflessness will make you feel good. Your newfound courage, wisdom, and empowerment will cause you to stand a little stronger than you did the day before. You will begin to build the belief that your story matters.

Making Lemonade

Lemon is one of my favorite flavors; right up there with chocolate. The interesting thing is that the lemon by itself is not palatable to most people. Lemons are sour. Think about sucking on a lemon right now, and I bet your mouth will water. You may even make a face. Lemons, however, when combined with other ingredients can be some of the most flavorful dishes.

It seemed for so long that I had nothing but lemons, so many that I joked that when I finally made lemonade, I would need a vat!

As you sit thinking about the "lemons" in your life, what can you add to them in order to create your unique recipe. What tools can you use to turn your handful, pile, or vat of lemons into your own unique lemonade?

There is a special lemonade recipe only you can create. Only one person has lived the life that you have lived and experienced what you have experienced. Therefore, your lemonade will have different ingredients than anybody else's.

Let's have a little fun with this. It is time to create your own unique Lemonade Recipe. The only food item in your recipe will be the lemons. They will symbolize the mountain you are climbing, the struggles you are in the process of overcoming. The lemons are a not-so-welcome gift from your Beast.

The remaining ingredients are the qualities, attributes, experiences, talents, knowledge, wisdom, humor, faith, courage, and strength you already have and those you are developing during your Battle.

The tools you will use to create your lemonade are the Nine Actions to Battle Your Beast.

Here is my personal recipe:

Valerie's Meaning From the Madness Lemonade

Ingredients:

- Vat of lemons
- Massive dose of humor
- Heaping helping of quick wit
- Truckload of love
- Big strainer of faith (it is in a strainer because it fell through the holes a few times)
- Steady stream of focus

Tools:

- Spiritual Armor (God)
- Oxygen Mask (so I can keep breathing)
- Circle of Strength (my people)
- Attitude Adjustor (for smacking myself upside the head when mine gets out of whack)
- Focus Binoculars (they only focus when pointed at the right things)
- Control Sifter (sifts out the stuff I can't control)
- Scaffolding (makes sure I am standing on top of my story, and not in it)

Mix the ingredients together, in no particular order. This recipe is flexible. It can be made with just a few ingredients or tools. Do not wait for all of the ingredients or tools, to whip up a batch. It will not be perfect, but neither is life. You can always come back and add the other ingredients, or use more tools later. Each time you adjust the recipe, it will get better and better.

Now it's your turn to make your Lemonade recipe. Have fun with it!

Well Done

Some of us have taken the harder road through life. Mine has been exciting, weary, confident, uncertain, courageous, terrifying, unpredictable, disciplined, meaningful, meaningless, fun, heartbreaking, hopeful, comfortable, uncomfortable, painful, manageable, and out of control.

"Life should not be a journey to the grave with the intention of arriving safely in a pretty and well-preserved body, but rather to skid in broadside in a cloud of smoke, thoroughly used up, totally worn out, and loudly proclaiming, "Wow! What a Ride!"
— Hunter S. Thompson

One day I will skid broadside in a cloud of smoke, totally worn out, and my ride will be over. Someday your ride will be over too. When mine is over and I stand at the gates of heaven, first I hope my name will be on the list! Assuming the gate angel finds my name, I will be called to stand before my maker for a little trip down my life's memory lane.

I'm sort of hoping God and I don't really have to watch the movie together; after all, we have both seen it. Is it really necessary to go over every gory detail again?

If we do, there will be scenes in my life story that will cause me to cover my eyes, to plug my ears. I may have to watch much of it peeking through my fingers. As the scenes of my life unfold, God will smile, and a time or two he will no doubt chuckle. He may downright laugh out loud.

During certain scenes, God might close his eyes or shake his head. While watching others, tears will stream down both of our cheeks. As the last scene flashes by and the credits roll, I will look sheepishly at God, holding my breath in anticipation of what he might say.

My hope and prayer is that when all things are taken into consideration he will whisper,

"Well done."

When the credits roll on your life's movie, it won't necessarily matter how it began or what happened near the middle. It isn't important whether your story was a serious drama, a comedy or a real tear-jerker. What matters is there is still time to change. If you're breathing, you still have time to add more scenes to your life's movie; to Make Meaning from the Madness.

278

Maybe you don't even believe in God. Still, at the end of our lives we all want to know that someone, somewhere, will think or say, "Well Done."

Fitting the Pieces Together

Understanding you can **Make Meaning From the Madness** gives you hope, and therefore you will be more likely to **Decide to Stand Up and Fight.** Knowing your life is bigger than you will help you to **Get On Your Spiritual Armor** and **Build Your Circle of Strength.** Realizing the opportunity to make meaning, you will want to **Change Your Attitude** and **Adjust Your Focus,** which will give you the courage to **Put On Your Oxygen Mask** and

Stand <u>On</u> Your Story. The realization that you're not the only person to have ridden the Roller Coaster from Hell will provide perspective to help you to **Stop Being a Control Freak.**

Battle Reminders

You may not be able to change what has happened, but you can make meaning from your story.

People are watching you, looking to be inspired, encouraged, and empowered.

You don't have to be Mother Teresa to make a difference.

Little things are big things.

Make some lemonade from your lemons.

Well Done.

Keeping the Pieces Together

You are probably wondering if I have my happy ending. The answer is, no. At the time of print, Jordan is still in the belly of her Beast. During the past year, I had her back and lost her again a couple of times. Drug addiction is a lifelong disease, so it is reasonable that my battle will be a lifelong battle to some degree. I'm prepared for that.

I continue to pray for her safety; for a thousand angels to surround and protect her. I also pray she hits rock bottom in whatever way is necessary for her to find the will to stand up and Battle her Beast.

When she is ready, I will be here to show her the way. Yes, she needs professional help I am in no position to provide. However, I can tell Jordan without reservation, that I have battled one helluva Beast. I fought my Beast after my heart had been broken into a million pieces. I stood up and took my life back while a dark cloud hung over my scarred heart.

I'm not here to tell you it has been easy or that I haven't stumbled, even before the ink was dry on this book. My Beast has done everything he can to stick his foot back into the doorway of my life. The forces of darkness have knocked me down but only to my knees. It is there on my knees that I continue to find the strength to stand up. What keeps me from allowing my Beast back, are the Actions in this book, which I still use every day.

I hope I am alive to witness Jordan's Battle; it will be epic. I picture the scene. Jordan's Beast is down on the mat; she is standing over him, and he is not getting back up. She has dealt the final blow. Although she is bruised, scarred, and bloodied, Jordan is the one standing. Slowly she turns around and takes a step into her future.

In the meantime, how do I keep the pieces of my heart together? I use the very actions in this book on a daily basis. They are daily lifelong actions.

If I can do this, you can too. You have what it takes to battle your Beast, whatever that Beast may be. You possess more courage, strength and wisdom than you give yourself credit for having. When you look to your right, or to your left, I hope you can picture me standing shoulder to shoulder with you.

Please visit us at www. RockinRedhead.com

Jordan, no matter where you are, where you go, or what you have done, I remain thankful God chose me to be your mom. I wish your life's path were easier, and I pray you find your way back from the belly of your Beast.

I will never stop believing in you, or loving you, and look forward to the day when I can stand with you while you choose life.

The Workbook is now available at Amazon.com

STILL STANDING
AFTER ALL THE TEARS

STRENGTH
MEANING
SELF LOVE
FAITH
DECIDE
CONTROL
STAND UP
FOCUS
ATTITUDE

Nine Actions to Battle Your Beast

WORKBOOK

Valerie Silveira

References

[i] "Codependent No More: How to Stop Controlling Others and Start Caring for Yourself" by Melody Beattie

[ii] http://www.merriam-webster.com/dictionary/enabler

[iii] http://www.ibisworld.com/industry/psychic-services.html

[iv] http://www.prweb.com/releases/2012/5/prweb9538067.htm

[v] http://content.time.com/time/health/article/0,8599,1912687,00.html

[vi] http://www.webmd.com/depression/guide/exercise-depression

[vii] Source: http://www.mayoclinic.org/stress-relief/art-20044456

[viii] "Codependent No More: How to Stop Controlling Others and Start Caring for Yourself" by Melody Beattie

[ix] Dictionary.com

CPSIA information can be obtained
at www.ICGtesting.com
Printed in the USA
FSOW02n2048130616
21509FS

9 780986 110405